CHRIST'S
GLORIOUS
ACHIEVEMENTS

C. H. SPURGEON

Christian Focus Publications Ltd.

© Christian Focus Publications Ltd.

ISBN 1 871676 28 2

Published by Christian Focus Publications Ltd.
Geanies House,
Fearn, Ross-shire,
IV20 1TW
Scotland, U.K.

Contents

PREFACE

This little volume consists of seven discourses in honour of our Lord Jesus. Upon no theme is the true minister so much at home, and yet no subject more completely surpasses his ability. We love the subject, though we are lost in it. It is possible to describe all other things more or less accurately; but words are not capable of setting forth the redeeming grace and dying love of Jesus: yet we would fain be confined to this one topic for life, and be set free to speak of nothing else but our Beloved. As the harp of Anacreon refused all other themes and would resound 'love alone', so would we gladly become for ever silent save only upon the famous deeds and adorable person of our Lord. 'Arms and THE MAN' we sing, but ah how feebly! Certainly we can never speak well enough of him whose name is Wonderful, for his work is honourable and glorious and his righteousness endureth for ever. We cannot content ourselves with anything which we can write concerning him, for, as the pen glides along, the heart glows yet more and more.

> 'My Christ he is the Lord of lords,
>   He is the King of kings
> He is the Sun of righteousness
>   With healing in his wings.
>
> My Christ, he is the heaven of heaven,
>   My Christ what shall I call?
> My Christ is first, my Christ is last,
>   My Christ is All in All.'

May the readers of these sermons be enabled by the Spirit of God in some degree to make increase in their knowledge of Christ. He alone is worth knowing; all other wisdom will fade away. Right well we know that none can reveal Christ to the heart but the Holy Ghost, and therefore with prayer for his divine enlightening we commit these pages to his condescending care, asking that they may prove to be good for edification. May the Lord Jesus be glorified by this little work.

Thus humbly prays:
C. H. SPURGEON

CHRIST
THE END OF THE LAW

For Christ is the end of the law for righteousness to every one that believeth.' – Romans 10:4

To be the end of the law is one of the most glorious achievements of our Lord, and it will be a great blessing to us all to know him in that character.

The reason why many do not come to Christ is not because they are not in earnest, after a fashion, and thoughtful, and desirous to be saved, but because they cannot brook God's way of salvation. Read the chapter from which the text is taken, and you will see that 'they have a zeal for God, but not according to knowledge.' We get them by our exhortations so far on the way that they become desirous to obtain eternal life, but 'they have not submitted themselves to the righteousness of God.' Mark, 'submitted themselves,' for it needs submission. Proud man wants to save himself, he believes he can do it, and he will not give over the task till he finds out his own helplessness by unhappy failures. Salvation by grace, to be asked for as an undeserved boon from free, unmerited favour, this it is which the carnal mind will not come to as long as it can help it: I beseech the Holy Spirit so to work that you may not be able to help it. I have been praying that, while I am trying to set forth Christ as the end of the law, God may bless it to some hearts, that they may see what Christ did, and may perceive it to be a great deal better than anything they can do; may see what Christ finished, and may become weary of what they themselves have laboured at so long, and have not even well commenced at this day. Perhaps it may please the Lord to enchant them with the perfection of the salvation that is in Christ Jesus. As Bunyan would say, 'It may, perhaps, set their mouths a-watering after it,' and when a sacred appetite begins, it will not be long before the feast is enjoyed. It may be that when they see the raiment of wrought gold, which Jesus so freely bestows on naked souls, they will throw away their own filthy rags which now they hug so closely.

I am going to speak about two things, as the Spirit of God shall help me: and the first is, *Christ in connection with the law* – he is 'the end of the law for righteousness;' and secondly, *ourselves in connection with Christ* – 'to everyone that believeth, Christ is the end of the law for righteousness.'

1. First, then, CHRIST IN CONNECTION WITH THE LAW. The law is that which as sinners, we have above all things cause to dread; for the sting of death is sin, and the strength of sin is the law. Towards us the law darts forth devouring flames, for it condemns us, and in solemn terms appoints us a place among the accursed, as it is written, 'Cursed is every one that continueth not in all things that are written in the book of the law to do them.' Yet, strange infatuation! Like the fascination which attracts the gnat to the candle, though it burns its wings, men by nature fly to the law for salvation, and cannot be kept from seeking life by it. The law can do nothing else but reveal sin and pronounce condemnation upon the sinner, and yet we cannot get men away from it, even though we show them how sweetly Jesus stands between them and it. They are so enamoured of legal hope that they cling to it when there is nothing to cling to; they prefer Sinai to Calvary, though Sinai has nothing for them but thunders and trumpet warnings of coming judgement. Oh, that for awhile you would listen anxiously while I set forth Jesus my Lord, that you may see the law fulfilled in him.

Now, what has our Lord to do with the law? He has everything to do with it, for he is its end for the noblest object, namely, for righteousness. He is 'the end of the law.' What does this mean? I think it signifies three things: first, that Christ is the *purpose and object* of the law; secondly, that he is *the fulfilment* of it; and thirdly, that he is *the termination* of it.

First, then, *our Lord Jesus Christ is the purpose and object of the law.* It was given to lead us to him. The law is our attendant to conduct us to the school of Jesus. The law is the great net in which the fish are enclosed that they may be drawn out of the element of sin. The law is the stormy wind which drives souls into the harbour of refuge. The law is the sheriff's officer to shut men up in prison for their sin, concluding them all under condemnation in order that they may look to the free grace of God alone for deliverance. This is the object of the law: it empties that grace may fill, and wounds that mercy may heal. It has never been God's intention towards us, as fallen men, that the law should be regarded as a way of salvation to us, for a way of salvation it can never be. Had man never fallen, had his nature remained as God made it, the law would have been most helpful to him to show him the way in which he should walk: and by keeping it he would have lived, for 'he that doeth these things shall live in them.' But ever since man has fallen the Lord has not proposed to him a way of salvation by works, for he knows it to be impossible to a sinful creature. The law is already broken; and whatever man can do he cannot repair the damage he has already done; therefore he is out of court as to the hope of merit. The law demands perfection, but man has already fallen short of it; and therefore let him do his best he cannot accomplish what is absolutely essential. The law is meant to lead the sinner to faith in Christ, by showing the impossibility of any other way. It is the black dog to fetch the sheep to the shepherd, the burning heat which drives the traveller to the shadow of the great rock in a weary land.

Look how the law is adapted to this; for, first of all, *it shows man his sin.* Read the ten commandments and tremble as you read them. Who can place his own character side by side with the two tablets of divine precepts without at once being convinced that he has fallen far short of the standard? When the law comes home to the soul it is like light in a dark room revealing the dust and the dirt which else had been unperceived. It is the test which detects the presence of the poison of sin in the soul. 'I was alive without the law once,' said the apostle, 'but when the commandment came sin revived and I died.' Our comeliness utterly fades away when the law blows upon it. Look at the commandments, I say, and remember how sweeping they are, how spiritual, how far-reaching. They do not merely touch the outward act, but dive into the inner motive and deal with the heart, the mind, the soul. There is a deeper meaning in the commands than appears upon their surface. Gaze into their depths and see how perfect is the holiness which they require. As you understand what the law demands, you will perceive how far you are from fulfilling it, and how sin abounds where you thought there was little or none of it. You thought yourself rich and increased in goods and in no need of anything, but when the broken law visits you, your spiritual bankruptcy and utter penury stare you in the face. A true balance discovers short weight, and such is the first effect of the law upon the conscience of man.

The law also shows *the result and mischief of sin.* Examine the types of the old Mosaic dispensation, and

see how they were intended to lead men to Christ by
making them see their unclean condition and their
need of such cleansing as only he can give. Every type
pointed to our Lord Jesus Christ. If men were put
apart because of disease or uncleanness, they were
made to see how sin separated them from God and
from his people; and when they were brought back
and purified with mystic rites in which were scarlet
wool and hyssop and the like, they were made to see
that they can only be restored by Jesus Christ, the
great High Priest. When the bird was killed that the
leper might be clean, the need of purification by the
sacrifice of a life was set forth. Every morning and
evening a lamb died to tell of daily need of pardon, if
God is to dwell with us. We sometimes have fault
found with us for speaking too much about blood; yet
under the old testament the blood was everything, and
was not only spoken of, but actually presented to the
eye. What does the apostle tell us in the Hebrews?
'Whereupon neither the first testament was dedicated
without blood. For when Moses had spoken every
precept to all the people according to the law, he took
the blood of calves and of goats, with water, and
scarlet wool, and hyssop, and sprinkled both the book
and all the people saying, This is the blood of the
testament which God hath enjoined unto you. Moreover he sprinkled with blood both the tabernacle, and
all the vessels of the ministry. And almost all things
are by the law purged with blood; and without shed-
ding of blood is no remission.' The blood was on the
veil, and on the altar, on the hangings, and on the
floor of the tabernacle: no one could avoid seeing it. I
resolve to make my ministry of the same character,
and more and more sprinkle it with the blood of
atonement. Now the abundance of the blood of old
was meant to show clearly that sin has so polluted

us that without an atonement God is not to be approached: we must come by the way of sacrifice, or not at all. We are so unacceptable in ourselves that unless the Lord sees us with the blood of Jesus upon us he must away with us. The old law, with its emblems and figures, set forth many truths as to men's selves and the coming Saviour, intending by every one of them to preach Christ. If any stopped short of him, they missed the intent and design of the law. Moses leads up to Joshua, and the law ends at Jesus.

Turning our thoughts back again to the moral rather than the ceremonial law, it was intended to teach men *their utter helplessness*. It shows them how utterly impossible it is for them to come up to the standard. Such holiness as the law demands no man can reach of himself. 'Thy commandment is exceeding broad.' If a man says that he can keep the law, it is because he does not know what the law is. If he fancies that he can ever climb to heaven up the quivering sides of Sinai, surely he can never have seen that burning mount at all. Keep the law! Ah, my brethren, while we are yet talking about it we are breaking it; while we are pretending that we can fulfil its letter, we are violating its spirit, for pride as much breaks the law as lust or murder. 'Who can bring a clean thing out of an unclean? Not one.' 'How can he be clean that is born of a woman?' No, soul, thou canst not help thyself in this thing, for since only by perfection thou canst live by the law, and since that perfection is impossible, thou canst not find help in the covenant of works. In grace there is hope, but as a matter of debt there is none, for we do not merit anything but wrath. The law tells us this, and the sooner we know it to be so the better, for the sooner we shall fly to Christ.

The law also shows us *our great need* – our need of cleansing, cleansing with the water and with the blood. It discovers to us our filthiness, and this naturally leads us to feel that we must be washed from it if we are ever to draw near to God. So the law drives us to accept of Christ as the only person who can cleanse us, and make us fit to stand within the veil in the presence of the Most High. The law is the surgeon's knife which cuts out the proud flesh that the wound may heal. The law by itself only sweeps and raises the dust, but the gospel sprinkles clean water upon the dust, and all is well in the chamber of the soul. The law kills, the gospel makes alive; the law strips, and then Jesus Christ comes in and robes the soul in beauty and glory. All the commandments and the types direct us to Christ, if we will but heed their evident intent. They wean us from self, they put us off from the false basis of self-righteousness and bring us to know that only in Christ can our help be found. So, first of all, Christ is the end of the law, in that he is its great purpose.

And now, secondly, he is *the law's fulfilment*. It is impossible for any of us to be saved without righteousness. The God of heaven and earth by immutable necessity demands righteousness of all his creatures. Now, Christ has come to give to us the righteousness which the law demands, but which it never bestows.

In the chapter before us we read of 'the righteousness which is of faith,' which is also called 'God's righteousness;' and we read of those who 'shall not be ashamed,' because they are righteous by believing, 'for with the heart man believeth unto righteousness.' What the law could not do Jesus has done. He provides the righteousness which the law asks for but cannot produce. What an amazing righteousness it must be which is as broad and deep and long and high as the law itself! The commandment is exceeding broad, but the righteousness of Christ is as broad as the commandment, and goes to the end of it. Christ did not come to make the law milder, or to render it possible for our cracked and battered obedience to be accepted as a sort of compromise. The law is not compelled to lower its terms, as though it had originally asked too much; it is holy and just and good, and ought not to be altered in one jot or tittle, nor can it be. Our Lord gives the law all it requires; not a part, for that would be an admission that it might justly have been content with less at first. The law claims complete obedience without one spot or speck, failure or flaw, and Christ has brought in such a righteousness as that, and has given it to his people. The law demands that the righteousness should be without omission of duty and without commission of sin, and the righteousness which Christ has brought in is just such an one that for its sake the great God accepts his people and counts them to be without spot or wrinkle or any such thing. The law will not be content without spiritual obedience; mere outward compliances will not satisfy.

But our Lord's obedience was as deep as it was broad, for his zeal to do the will of him that sent him consumed him. He says himself, 'I delight to do thy will, O my God, yea thy law is within my heart.' Such righteousness he puts upon all believers. 'By the obedience of one shall many be made righteous;' righteous to the full; perfect in Christ. We rejoice to wear the costly robe of fair white linen which Jesus has prepared, and we feel that we may stand arrayed in it before the Majesty of heaven without a trembling thought. This is something to dwell upon, dear friends. Only as righteous ones can we be saved, but Jesus Christ makes us righteous, and therefore we are saved. He is righteous who believeth on him, even as

Abraham believed God and it was counted unto him for righteousness. 'There is, therefore, now no condemnation to them that are in Christ Jesus,' because they are made righteous in Christ. Yea, the Holy Spirit by the mouth of Paul challengeth all men, angels, and devils, to lay anything to the charge of God's elect, since Christ hath died. O law, when thou demandest of me a perfect righteousness, I, being a believer, present it to thee; for through Christ Jesus faith is accounted unto me for righteousness. The righteousness of Christ is mine, for I am one with him by faith, and this is the name wherewith he shall be called – 'The Lord our righteousness.'

Jesus has thus fulfilled the original demands of the law, but you know, brethren, that since we have broken the law there are other demands. For the remission of past sins something more is asked now than present and future obedience. Upon us, on account of our sins, the curse has been pronounced, and a penalty has been incurred. It is written that he 'will by no means clear the guilty,' but every transgression and iniquity shall have its just punishment and reward. Here, then, let us admire that the Lord Jesus Christ is the end of the law as to penalty. That curse and penalty are awful things to think upon, but Christ has ended all their evil, and thus discharged us from all the consequences of sin. As far as every believer is concerned the law demands no penalty and utters no curse. The believer can point to the Great Surety on the tree of Calvary, and say, 'See there, oh law, there is the vindication of divine justice which I offer to thee! Jesus pouring out his heart's blood from his wounds, and dying on my behalf, is my answer to thy claims, and I know that I shall be delivered from wrath through him.' The claims of the law, both as broken and unbroken, Christ has met: both the positive and the penal demands are satisfied in him. This was a labour worthy of a God, and lo, the incarnate God has achieved it. He has finished the transgression, made an end of sins, made reconciliation for iniquity, and brought in everlasting righteousness. All glory be to his name.

Moreover, not only has the penalty been paid, but Christ has put great and special honour upon the law in so doing. I venture to say that if the whole human race had kept the law of God and not one of them had violated it, the law would not stand in so splendid a position of honour as it does today since the man Christ Jesus, who is also the Son of God, has paid obeisance to it. God himself, incarnate, has in his life, and yet more in his death, revealed the supremacy of law; he has shown that not even love nor sovereignty can set aside justice. Who shall say a word against the law to which the Lawgiver himself submits? Who shall now say that it is too severe, when he who made it submits himself to its penalties? Because he was found in fashion as a man, and was our representative, the Lord demanded from his own Son perfect obedience to the law, and the Son voluntarily bowed himself to it without a single word, taking no exception to his task. 'Yea, the law is my delight,' said he, and he proved it to be so by paying homage to it even to the full. Oh wondrous law under which even Immanuel serves! Oh matchless law whose yoke even the Son of God does not disdain to bear, but being resolved to save his chosen, was made under the law, lived under it and died under it, 'obedient to death, even the death of the cross.'

The law's stability also has been secured by Christ. That alone can remain which is proved to be just, and Jesus has proved the law to be so, magnifying it and making it honourable. He says, 'Think not that I am come to destroy the law or the prophets: I am not come to destroy, but to fulfil. For verily I say unto you, till heaven and earth pass, one jot or one tittle shall in no wise pass from the law, till all be fulfilled.' I shall have to show you how he has made an end of the law in another sense, but as to the settlement of the eternal principle of right and wrong, Christ's life and death have achieved this forever. 'Yea, we establish the law,' said Paul, 'we do not make void the law through faith.' The law is proved to be holy and just by the very gospel of faith, for the gospel which faith believes in does not alter or lower the law, but teaches us how it was to the uttermost fulfilled. Now shall the law stand fast for ever and ever, since even to save elect man God will not alter it. He had a people, chosen, beloved, and ordained to life, yet he would not save them at the expense of one principle of right. They were sinful, and how could they be justified unless the law was suspended or changed? Was, then, the law changed? It seemed as if it must be so, if man was to be saved, but Jesus Christ came and showed us how the law could stand firm as a rock, and yet the redeemed could be justly saved by infinite mercy. In Christ we see both mercy and justice shining full orbed, and yet neither of them in any degree eclipsing the other. The law has all it ever asked, as it ought to have, and yet the Father of all mercies sees all his chosen saved as he determined they should be through the death of his Son. Thus I have tried to show you how Christ is the fulfilment of the law to its utmost end. May the Holy Ghost bless the teaching.

And now, thirdly, he is the end of the law in the sense that he is *the termination of it*. He has terminated it in two senses. First of all, his people are not under it as a covenant of life. 'We are not under the law, but under grace.' The old covenant as it stood with father

Adam was 'This do and thou shalt live': its command he did not keep, and consequently he did not live, nor do we live in him, since in Adam all died. The old covenant was broken, and we became condemned thereby; but now, having suffered death in Christ, we are no more under it, but are dead to it. Brethren, at this present moment, although we rejoice to do good works, we are not seeking life through them, we are not hoping to obtain divine favour by our own goodness, nor even to keep ourselves in the love of God by any merit of our own. Chosen, not for our works, but according to the eternal will and good pleasure of God; called, not of works, but by the Spirit of God, we desire to continue in his grace and return no more to the bondage of the old covenant. Since we have put our trust in an atonement provided and applied by grace through Christ Jesus, we are no longer slaves, but children, not working to be saved, but saved already, and working because we are saved. Neither that which we do, nor even that which the Spirit of God worketh in us is to us the ground and basis of the love of God toward us, since he loved us from the first, because he would love us, unworthy though we were; and he loves us still in Christ, and looks upon us not as we are in ourselves, but as we are in him, washed in his blood and covered with his righteousness. Ye are not under the law, Christ has taken you from the servile bondage of a condemning covenant and made you to receive the adoption of children, so that now ye cry, Abba, Father.

Again, Christ is the terminator of the law, for we are no longer under its curse. The law cannot curse a believer, it does not know how to do it; it blesses him, yea, and he shall be blessed; for as the law demands righteousness and looks at the believer in Christ, and sees that Jesus has given him all the righteousness it demands, the law is bound to pronounce him blessed. 'Blessed is he whose transgression is forgiven, whose sin is covered. Blessed is the man unto whom the Lord imputeth not iniquity, and in whose spirit there is no guile.' Oh, the joy of being redeemed from the curse of the law by Christ, who was 'made a curse for us,' as it is written, 'Cursed is every one that hangeth on a tree.' Do ye, my brethren, understand the sweet mystery of salvation? Have you ever seen Jesus standing in your place that you may stand in his place? Christ accused and Christ condemned, and Christ led out to die, and Christ smitten of the Father, even to the death; and then, you cleared, justified, delivered from the curse, because the curse has spent itself on your Redeemer? You are admitted to enjoy the blessing because the righteousness which was his is now transferred to you that you may be blessed of the Lord world without end. Do let us triumph and rejoice in this evermore. Why should we not? And yet some of God's people get under the law as to their feelings, and begin to fear that because they are conscious of sin they are not saved, whereas it is written, 'he justifieth the ungodly.' For myself, I love to live near a sinner's Saviour. If my standing before the Lord depended upon what I am in myself and what good works and righteousness I could bring, surely I should have to condemn myself a thousand times a day. But to get away from that and to say, 'I have believed in Jesus Christ and therefore righteousness is mine,' this is peace, rest, joy, and the beginning of heaven! When one attains to this experience, his love to Jesus Christ begins to flame up, and he feels that if the Redeemer has delivered him from the curse of the law he will not continue in sin, but he will endeavour to live in newness of life. We are not our own, we are bought with a price, and we would therefore glorify God in our bodies and in our spirits which are the Lord's. Thus much upon Christ in connection with the law.

2. Now secondly, OURSELVES IN CONNECTION WITH CHRIST – for 'Christ is the end of the law *to every one that believeth.'* Now see the point – 'to every one that believeth,' there the stress lies. Come, man, woman, dost thou believe? No weightier question can be asked under heaven. 'Dost thou believe on the Son of God?' And what is it to believe? It is not merely to accept a set of doctrines and to say that such and such a creed is yours, and there and then to put it on the shelf and forget it. To believe is, to trust, to confide, to depend upon, to rely upon, to rest in. Dost thou believe that Jesus Christ rose from the dead? Dost thou believe that he stood in the sinner's stead and suffered the just for the unjust? Dost thou believe that he is able to save to the uttermost them that come unto God by him? And dost thou therefore lay the whole weight and stress of thy soul's salvation upon him, yea, upon him alone? Ah, then, Christ is the end of the law for righteousness to thee, and thou art righteous. In the righteousness of God thou art clothed if thou believest. It is of no use to bring forward anything else if you are not believing, for nothing will avail. If faith be absent, the essential thing is wanting: sacraments, prayers, Bible reading, hearings of the gospel, you may heap them together, high as the stars, into a mountain, huge as high Olympus, but they are all mere chaff if faith be not there. It is thy believing or not believing which must settle the matter. Dost thou look away from thyself to Jesus for righteousness? If thou dost he is the end of the law to thee.

Now observe that there is no question raised concerning previous character, for it is written, 'Christ is the end of the law for righteousness to *every one that believeth.*' But, Lord, this man before he believed was a persecutor and injurious, he raged and raved against the saints and haled them to prison and sought their blood. Yes, beloved friend, and that is the very man who wrote these words by the Holy Ghost, 'Christ is the end of the law for righteousness to every one that believeth.' So if I address an individual whose life has been defiled with every sin, and stained with every transgression, yet I say unto such, 'all manner of sin and of blasphemy shall be forgiven unto men.' If thou believest in the Lord Jesus Christ thine iniquities are blotted out; for the blood of Jesus Christ, God's dear Son, cleanseth us from all sin. It is the glory of the gospel that it is a sinner's gospel; good news of blessing not for those without sin, but for those who confess and forsake it. Jesus came into the world, not to reward the sinless, but to seek and to save that which was lost; and he, being lost and being far from God, who cometh nigh to God by Christ, and believeth in him, will find that he is able to bestow righteousness upon the guilty. He is the end of the law for righteousness to every one that believeth, and therefore to the poor harlot that believeth, to the drunkard of many years' standing that believeth, to the thief, the liar, and the scoffer who believeth, to those who have aforetime rioted in sin, but now turn from it to trust in him. But I do not know that I need mention such cases as these; to me the most wonderful fact is that Christ is the end of the law for righteousness to me, for I believe in him. I know whom I have believed, and I am persuaded that he is able to keep that which I have committed to him until that day.

Another thought arises from the text, and that is, that there is nothing said by way of qualification as to the strength of the faith. He is the end of the law for righteousness to *everyone* that believeth, whether he be Little Faith or Greatheart. Jesus protects the rear rank as well as the vanguard. There is no difference between one believer and another as to justification. So long as there is a connection between you and Christ, the righteousness of God is yours. The link may be very like a film, a mere spider's line of trembling faith, but, if it runs all the way from the heart to Christ, divine grace can and will flow along the most slender thread. It is marvellous how fine the wire may be that will carry the electric fluid. We need a cable to carry a message across the sea, but that is for the protection of the wire within. The wire which actually carries the message is a slender thing. If thy faith be of the mustard-seed kind, if it be only such as tremblingly touches the Saviour's garment's hem, if thou canst only say, 'Lord, I believe, help thou mine unbelief,' if it be but the faith of sinking Peter, or weeping Mary, yet if it be faith in Christ, he will be the end of the law for righteousness to thee as well as to the chief of the apostles.

If this be so, then, beloved friends, all of us who believe are righteous. Believing in the Lord Jesus Christ we have obtained the righteousness which those who follow the works of the law know nothing of. We are not completely sanctified, would God we were; we are not quit of sin in our members, though we hate it; but still for all that, in the sight of God we are truly righteous, and being justified by faith we have peace with God. Come, look up, ye believers who are burdened with a sense of sin. While you chasten yourselves and mourn your sins, do not doubt your Saviour, nor question his righteousness. You are black, but do not stop there, go on to say as the spouse did, 'I am black, but *comely.*'

'Though in ourselves deform'd we are,
  And black as Kedar's tents appear,
Yet, when we put thy beauties on,
  Fair as the court of Solomon.'

Now, mark that the connection of our text assures us that being righteous we are saved; for what does it say here? 'If thou shalt confess with thy mouth the Lord Jesus, and shalt believe in thine heart that God hath raised him from the dead, thou shalt be *saved.*' He who is justified is saved, or what were the benefit of justification? Over thee, O believer, God hath pronounced the verdict '*saved*' and none shall reverse it. You are saved from sin and death and hell; you are saved even now, with a present salvation, for it is written, 'He hath saved us and called us with a holy calling.' Feel the transports of salvation at this hour.

And now I have done when I have said just this. If any one thinks he can save himself, and that his own righteousness will suffice before God, I would affectionately beg him not to insult his Saviour. If your righteousness sufficeth, why did Christ come here to work one out? Will you for a moment compare your righteousness with the righteousness of Jesus Christ? What likeness is there between you and him? As much as between an emmet and an archangel. Nay, not so much as that: as much as between night and day, hell and heaven. Oh, if I had a righteousness of my own that no one could find fault with, I would voluntarily fling it away to have the righteousness of Christ, but as I have none of my own I do rejoice the more to have my Lord's. When Mr Whitefield first preached at Kingswood, near Bristol, to the colliers, he could see when their hearts began to be touched, by the gutters of white made by the tears as they ran down their black cheeks. He saw they were receiving the gospel, and he writes in his diary, 'As these poor colliers had no righteousness of their own they therefore gloried in him who came to save publicans and sinners.' Well, Mr Whitefield, that is true of the colliers, but it is equally true of many of us here, who may not have had black faces, but we had black hearts. We can truly say that we also rejoice to cast away our own righteousness and count it dross and dung that we may win Christ, and be found in him. In Jesus is our sole hope and only trust.

Last of all, for any of you to reject the righteousness of Christ must be to perish everlastingly, because it cannot be that God will accept you or your pretended righteousness when you have refused the real and divine righteousness which he sets before you in his Son. If you could go up to the gates of heaven, and the angel were to say to you, 'What title have you to entrance here?' and you were to reply, 'I have a righteousness of my own,' then for you to be admitted would be to decide that your righteousness was on a par with that of Immanuel himself. Can that ever be? Do you think that God will allow such a lie to be sanctioned? Will he let a poor wretched sinner's counterfeit righteousness pass current side by side with the fine gold of Christ's perfection? Why was the fountain filled with blood if you need no washing? Is Christ a superfluity? Oh, it cannot be. You must have Christ's righteousness or be unrighteous, and being unrighteous you will be unsaved, and being unsaved you must remain lost for ever and ever.

What! Has it come to this, that I am to believe in the Lord Jesus Christ for righteousness, and to be made just through faith? Yes, that is the whole of it. What! Trust Christ alone and then live as I like? You cannot live in sin after you have trusted Jesus, for the Spirit of God who leads you to believe will also change your heart.

You spoke of 'living as you like,' you will like to live very differently from what you do now. The things you loved before your conversion you will hate when you believe, and the things you hated you will love. Now you are trying to be good, and you make great failures because your heart is alienated from God; but when you have received salvation through the blood of Christ, your heart will love God, and then his commandments will no longer be grievous to you. A change of heart is what you want, and you will never get it except through the covenant of grace. There is not a word about conversion in the old covenant, we must look to the new covenant for that, and here it is – 'A new heart also will I give you, and a new spirit will I put within you: and I will take away the stony heart out of your flesh, and I will give you an heart of flesh.' This is one of the greatest covenant promises, and the Holy Ghost performs it in the chosen. Oh that the Lord would sweetly persuade you to believe in the Lord Jesus Christ, and that covenant promise shall be fulfilled to you. O Holy Spirit of God, send thy blessing on these poor words, for Jesus' sake.

CHRIST
THE CONQUEROR OF SATAN

'And I will put enmity between thee and the woman, and between thy seed and her seed; it shall bruise thy head, and thou shalt bruise his heel.' – Genesis 3:15.

We shall now consider the glorious achievements of our Lord Jesus as the Conqueror of that arch-enemy of man, the devil.

Our text is the first gospel sermon that was ever delivered upon this earth. It was a memorable discourse indeed, for it had Jehovah himself for the preacher, and the whole human race and the prince of darkness for the audience. It must be worthy of our heartiest attention.

Is it not remarkable that this great gospel promise should have been delivered so soon after the transgression? Not yet had the woman been condemned to painful travail, or the man to exhausting labour, or even the soil to the curse of thorn and thistle. Truly 'mercy rejoiceth against judgment.' Before the Lord had said, 'Dust thou art and unto dust thou shalt return,' he was pleased to say that the seed of the woman should bruise the serpent's head. Let us rejoice in the swift mercy of God, which in the early watches of the night of sin came with comfortable words unto us.

These words were not directly spoken to Adam and Eve, but they were directed to the serpent himself, and that by way of punishment to him for what he had done. It was a day of cruel triumph to him: such joy as his dark mind is capable of had filled him, for he had indulged his malice, and gratified his spite. He had destroyed a part of God's works, he had introduced sin into the new world, he had stamped the human race with his own image, and gained new forces to promote rebellion, and therefore he felt that sort of gladness which a fiend can know who bears a hell within him. But now God comes in, takes up the quarrel personally, and causes him to be disgraced on the very battlefield upon which he had gained a temporary success. He tells the enemy that he will undertake to deal with him; this quarrel shall not be between the serpent and man, but between God and the serpent. God saith, in solemn words, 'I will put enmity between thee and the woman, between thy seed and her seed,' and he promises that there shall rise in fulness of time a champion, who, though he suffer shall smite in a vital part the power of evil, and bruise the serpent's head. This was the more, it seems to me, a comfortable message of mercy to Adam and Eve, because they would feel sure that the tempter would be punished, and as that punishment would involve blessing for them, the vengeance due to the serpent would be the guarantee of mercy to themselves. Perhaps, however, by thus obliquely giving the promise, the Lord meant to say, 'Not for your sakes do I this, O fallen man and woman, but for my own name and honour's sake, that it be not blasphemed amongst the fallen spirits, I undertake to repair the mischief which has been caused by the tempter.' All this would be very humbling but very consolatory to our parents, seeing that mercy given for God's sake is always to our troubled apprehension more sure than any favour which could be promised to us for our own sake. The divine sovereignty and glory afford us a stronger foundation of hope than merit, even if merit can be supposed to exist.

We must note concerning this first gospel sermon that on it the earliest believers stayed themselves. This was all that Adam had by way of revelation. This lone star shone in Abel's sky; he looked up to it and by its light he spelt out 'sacrifice,' and therefore he brought of the firstlings of his flock and laid them upon the altar, and proved in his own person how the seed of the serpent hated the seed of the woman, for his brother slew him for his testimony. Although Enoch the seventh from Adam prophesied concerning the second advent, yet he does not appear to have uttered anything new concerning the first coming, so that still this one promise remained as man's sole word of hope. The torch which flamed within the gates of Eden just before man was driven forth lit up the world to all believers until the Lord was pleased to give more light, and to renew and enlarge the revelation of his covenant, when he spake to his servant Noah. Those hoary fathers who lived before the flood rejoiced in the mysterious language of our text, and resting on it, they died in faith.

Nor must we think it a slender revelation, for, if we attentively consider, it is full of meaning. If it had been on my heart to handle it doctrinally this morning, I think I could have shown you that it contains all the gospel. There lie within it, as an oak lies within an acorn, all the great truths which make up the gospel of Christ. Observe that there is the grand mystery of the incarnation. Christ is that seed of the woman who is here spoken of; and there is a hint not darkly given as to how that incarnation would be effected. Jesus was not born after ordinary manner of the sons of men. Mary was overshadowed of the Holy Ghost, and 'the holy thing' which was born of her was as to his humanity the seed of the woman only; as it is written, 'Behold, a virgin shall conceive and bear a son, and they shall call his name Immanuel.' The promise plainly teaches that the deliverer would be born of a woman, and, carefully viewed, it also foreshadows the divine method of the Redeemer's conception and birth. So also is the doctrine of the two seeds plainly taught here – 'I will put enmity between thee and the woman, between thy seed and her seed.' There was evidently to be in the world a seed of the woman on God's side against the serpent, and a seed of the serpent that should always be upon the evil side even as it is unto this day. The church of God and the synagogue of Satan both exist. We see an Abel and a Cain, an Isaac and an Ishmael, a Jacob and an Esau; those that are born after the flesh, being the children of their father the devil, for his works they do, but those that are born again – being born after the Spirit, are thus in Christ Jesus the seed of the woman, and contend earnestly against the dragon and his seed. Here, too, the great fact of the sufferings of Christ is clearly foretold – 'Thou shalt bruise his heel.' Within the compass of those words we find the whole story of our Lord's sorrows from Bethlehem to Calvary. 'It shall bruise thy head': there is the breaking of Satan's regal power, there is the clearing away of sin, there is the destruction of death by resurrection, there is the leading captivity captive in the ascension, there is the victory of truth in the world through the descent of the Spirit, and there is the latter-day glory in which Satan shall be bound, and there is, lastly, the casting of the evil one and all his followers into the lake of fire. The conflict and the conquest are both in the compass of these few fruitful words. They may not have been fully understood by those who first heard them, but to us they are now full of light. The text at first looks like a flint, hard and cold; but sparks fly from it plentifully, for hidden fires of infinite love and grace lie concealed within. Over this promise of a gracious God we ought to rejoice exceedingly.

We do not know what our first parents understood

by it, but we may be certain that they gathered a great amount of comfort from it. They must have perceived that they were not then and there to be destroyed, because the Lord had spoken of a 'seed.' They would argue that it must be needful that Eve should live if there should be a seed from her. They felt, too, that some mysterious benefit was to be conferred upon them by the victory which their seed would achieve over the instigator of their ruin. They went on in faith upon this, and were comforted in travail and in toil, and I doubt not both Adam and his wife in the faith thereof entered into everlasting rest.

This morning I intend to handle this text in three ways. First, we shall notice *its facts;* secondly, we shall consider, *the experience within the heart of each believer which tallies to those facts;* and then, thirdly, *the encouragement* which the text and its connection as a whole afford to us.

1. THE FACTS. The facts are four, and I call your earnest attention to them. The first is, *Enmity was excited.* The text begins, 'I will put enmity between thee and the woman.' They had been very friendly: the woman and the serpent had conversed together. She thought at the time that the serpent was her friend; and she was so much his friend that she took his advice in the teeth of God's precept, and was willing to believe bad things of the great Creator, because this wicked, crafty serpent insinuated the same. Now, at the moment when God spake, that friendship between the woman and the serpent had already in a measure come to an end, for she had accused the serpent to God, and said, 'The serpent beguiled me, and I did eat.' So far, so good. The friendship of sinners does not last long; they have already begun to quarrel, and now the Lord comes in and graciously takes advantage of the quarrel which had commenced, and says, 'I

will carry this disagreement further, I will put enmity between thee and the woman.' Satan counted on man's descendants being his confederates, but God would break up this covenant with hell, and raise up a seed which should war against the Satanic power. Thus we have here God's first declaration that he will set up a rival kingdom to oppose the tyranny of sin and Satan, and that he will create in the hearts of a chosen seed an enmity against evil, so that they shall fight against it, and with many a struggle and pain shall overcome the prince of darkness. The divine Spirit has abundantly achieved this purpose of the Lord, combating the fallen angel by a glorious man: making man to be Satan's foe and conqueror. Henceforth the woman was to hate the evil one, and doubtless she did so. She had abundant cause for so doing, and as often as she thought of him, it would be with infinite regret that she could have listened to his deceitful talk. The woman's seed has also evermore had enmity against the evil one. I mean not the carnal seed, for Paul tells us, 'They which are the children of the flesh, these are not the children of God: but the children of the promise are counted for the seed.' The carnal seed are not meant, but the spiritual seed, even Christ Jesus and those who are in him. Wherever you meet these, they hate the serpent with a perfect hatred.

We would, if we could, destroy from our souls every work of Satan, and out of this poor afflicted world of ours we would root up every evil which he has planted. That seed of the woman, that glorious *One* – for he speaks not of seeds as of many, but of seed that is one, – you know how he abhorred the devil and all his devices. There was enmity between Christ and Satan, for he came to destroy the works of the devil and to deliver those who are under bondage to him. For that purpose was he born; for that purpose did he live; for that purpose did he die; for that purpose he has gone into the glory, and for that purpose he will come again, that everywhere he may find out his adversary and utterly destroy him and his works from amongst the sons of men. This putting of the enmity between the two seeds was the commencement of the plan of mercy, the first act in the programme of grace. Of the woman's seed it was henceforth said, 'Thou lovest righteousness, and hatest wickedness: therefore God, thy God, hath anointed thee with the oil of gladness above thy fellows.'

Then comes the second prophecy, which has also turned into a fact, namely *the coming of the Champion*. The seed of the woman by promise is to champion her cause, and oppose the dragon. That seed is the Lord Jesus Christ. The prophet Micah saith, 'But thou, Bethlehem Ephratah, though thou be little among the thousands of Judah, yet out of thee shall he come forth unto me that is to be ruler in Israel; whose goings forth have been from of old, from everlasting. Therefore will he give them up, until the time that she which travaileth hath brought forth.' To none other than the babe which was born in Bethlehem of the blessed Virgin can the words of the prophecy refer. It is concerning her Son that we sing, 'Unto us a child is born, unto us a Son is given.' On the memorable night at Bethlehem, when angels sang in heaven, the seed of the woman appeared, and as soon as ever he saw the light, the old serpent, the devil, entered into the heart of Herod to slay him if possible, but the Father preserved him, and suffered none to lay hands on him. As soon as he publicly came forward upon the stage of action, thirty years after, Satan met him foot to foot. You know the story of the temptation in the wilderness, and how there the woman's seed fought with him

who was a liar from the beginning. The devil assailed
him thrice with all the artillery of flattery, malice,
craft and falsehood, but the peerless Champion stood
unwounded, and chased his foeman from the field.
Then our Lord set up his kingdom and called one and
another to him, and carried the war into the enemy's
country. In divers places he cast out devils. He spake
to the wicked and unclean spirit and said, 'I charge
thee come out of him,' and the demon was expelled.
Legions of devils flew before him: they sought to hide
themselves in swine to escape from the terror of his
presence. 'Art thou come to torment us before our
time?' was their cry when the wonder-working Christ
dislodged them from the bodies which they tormented.
Yea, and he made his own disciples mighty against the
evil one, for in his name they cast out devils, till Jesus
said, 'I beheld Satan as lightning fall from heaven.'
Then there came a second personal conflict, for I take
it that Gethsemane's sorrows were to a great degree
caused by a personal assault of Satan, for our Master
said, 'This is your hour, and the power of darkness.'
He said also, 'The prince of this world cometh.' What
a struggle it was! Though Satan had nothing in Christ,
yet did he seek if possible to draw him away from
completing his great sacrifice, and there did our
Master sweat as it were great drops of blood, falling to
the ground, in the agony which it cost him to contend
with the fiend. Then it was that our Champion began
the last fight of all and won it to the bruising of the
serpent's head. Nor did he end till he had spoiled
principalities and powers and made a show of them
openly.

    'Now is the hour of darkness past,
       Christ has assumed his reigning power;
     Behold the great accuser cast
       Down from his seat to reign no more.'

The conflict, our glorious Lord continues in his seed. We preach Christ crucified, and every sermon shakes the gates of hell. We bring sinners to Jesus by the Spirit's power, and every convert is a stone torn down from the wall of Satan's mighty castle. Yea, and the day shall come when everywhere the evil one shall be overcome and the words of John in the Revelation shall be fulfilled: 'And the great dragon was cast out, that old serpent, called the Devil, and Satan, which deceiveth the whole world: he was cast out into the earth, and his angels were cast out with him. And I heard a loud voice saying in heaven, Now is come salvation, and strength, and the kingdom of our God, and the power of his Christ: for the accuser of our brethren is cast down, which accused them before our God day and night.' Thus did the Lord God in the words of our text promise a Champion who should be the seed of the woman, between whom and Satan there should be war for ever and ever: that Champion has come, the man-child has been born, and though the dragon is wroth with the woman, and makes war with the remnant of her seed which keep the testimony of Jesus Christ, yet the battle is the Lord's and the victory falleth unto him whose name is Faithful and True, who in righteousness doth judge and make war.

The third fact which comes out in the text, though not quite in that order, is that *our Champion's heel should be bruised*. Do you need that I explain this? You know how all his life long his heel, that is, his lower part, his human nature, was perpetually being made to suffer. He carried our sicknesses and sorrows. But the bruising came mainly when both in body and in mind his whole human nature was made to agonise; when his soul was exceeding sorrowful even unto death, and his enemies pierced his hands and his feet, and he endured the shame and pain of death by crucifixion. Look at your Master and your King upon the cross, all distained with blood and dust! There was his heel most cruelly bruised. When they take down that precious body and wrap it in fair white linen and in spices, and lay it in Joseph's tomb, they weep as they handle that casket in which the Deity had dwelt, for there again Satan had bruised his heel. It was not merely that God had bruised him, 'though it pleased the Father to bruise him,' but the devil had let loose Herod, and Pilate, and Caiaphas, and the Jews, and the Romans, all of them his tools, upon him whom he knew to be the Christ, so that he was bruised of the old serpent. That is all, however! It is only his heel, not his head, which is bruised! For lo, the Champion rises again; the bruise was not mortal nor continual. Though he dies, yet still so brief is the interval in which he slumbers in the tomb that his holy body hath not seen corruption, and he comes forth perfect and lovely in his manhood, rising from his grave as from a refreshing sleep after so long a day of unresting toil! Oh the triumph of that hour! As Jacob only halted on his thigh when he overcame the angel, so did Jesus only retain a scar in his heel, and that he bears to the skies as his glory and beauty. Before the throne he looks like a lamb that has been slain, but in the power of an endless life he liveth unto God.

Then comes the fourth fact, namely, that while his heel was being bruised, *he was to bruise the serpent's head.* The figure represents the dragon as inflicting an injury upon the Champion's heel, but at the same moment the Champion himself with that heel crushes in the head of the serpent with fatal effect. By his sufferings Christ has overthrown Satan, by the heel that was bruised he has trodden upon the head which devised the bruising.

'Lo, by the sons of hell he dies;
  But as he hangs 'twixt earth and skies,
He gives their prince a fatal blow,
  And triumphs o'er the powers below.'

Though Satan is not dead, my brethren, I was about to say, would God he were, and though he is not converted, and never will be, nor will the malice of his heart ever be driven from him, yet Christ has so far broken his head that he has missed his mark altogether. He intended to make the human race the captives of his power, but they are redeemed from his iron yoke. God has delivered many of them, and the day shall come when he will cleanse the whole earth from the serpent's slimy trail, so that the entire world shall be full of the praises of God. He thought that this world would be the arena of his victory over God and good, instead of which it is already the grandest theatre of divine wisdom, love, grace and power. Even heaven itself is not so resplendent with mercy as the earth is, for here it is the Saviour poured out his blood, which cannot be said even of the courts of paradise above. Moreover, he thought, no doubt, that when he had led our race astray and brought death upon them, he had effectually marred the Lord's work. He rejoiced that they would all pass under the cold seal of death, and that their bodies would rot in the sepulchre. Had he not spoiled the handiwork of his great Lord? God may make man as a curious creature with intertwisted veins and blood nerves, and sinews and muscles, and he may put into his nostrils the breath of life; but, 'Ah,' saith Satan, 'I have infused a poison into him which will make him return to the dust from which he was taken.' But now, behold, our Champion whose heel was bruised has risen from the dead, and given us a pledge that all his followers shall

36

rise from the dead also. Thus is Satan foiled, for death shall not retain a bone, nor a piece of a bone, of one of those who belonged to the woman's seed. At the trump of the archangel from the earth and from the sea they shall arise, and this shall be their shout, 'O death, where is thy sting? O grave, where is thy victory?' Satan, knowing this, feels already that by the resurrection his head is broken. Glory be to the Christ of God for this!

In multitudes of other ways the devil has been vanquished by our Lord Jesus, and so shall he ever be till he shall be cast into the lake of fire.

2. Let us now view **OUR EXPERIENCE AS IT TALLIES WITH THESE FACTS.** We were by nature, as many of us as have been saved, the heirs of wrath even as others. It does not matter how godly our parents were, the first birth brought us no spiritual life, for the promise is not to them which are born of blood, or of the will of the flesh, or of the will of man, but only those who are born of God. 'That which is born of the flesh is flesh;' you cannot make it anything else and there it abides, and the flesh, or carnal mind, abideth in death; 'it is not reconciled to God, neither indeed can be.' He who is born into this world but once, and knows nothing of the new birth, must place himself among the seed of the serpent, for only by regeneration can we know ourselves to be the true seed. How does God deal with us who are his called and chosen ones? He means to save us, and how does he work to that end?

The first thing he does is, he come to us in mercy, and *puts enmity between us and the serpent*. That is the first work of grace. There was peace between us and Satan once; when he tempted we yielded; whatever he taught us we believed; we were his willing slaves. But perhaps you, my brethren, can recollect when first of all you began to feel uneasy and dissatisfied; the world's pleasures no longer pleased you; all the juice seemed to have been taken out of the apple, and you had nothing left but the hard core, which you could not feed upon at all. Then you suddenly perceived that you were living in sin, and you were miserable about it, and though you could not get rid of sin yet you hated it, and sighed over it, and cried, and groaned. In your heart of hearts you remained no longer on the side of evil, for you began to cry, 'O wretched man that I am, who shall deliver me from the body of this death?' You were already from of old in the covenant of grace ordained to be the woman's seed, and now the decree began to discover itself in life bestowed upon you and working in you. The Lord in infinite mercy dropped the divine life into your soul. You did not know it, but there it was, a spark of the celestial fire, the living and incorruptible seed which abideth for ever. You began to hate sin, and you groaned under it as under a galling yoke; more and more it burdened you, you could not bear it, you hated the very thought of it. So it was with you: is it so now? Is there still enmity between you and the serpent? Indeed you are more and more the sworn enemies of evil and you willingly acknowledge it.

Then came the Champion: that is to say, 'Christ was formed in you the hope of glory.' You heard of him and you understood the truth about him, and it seemed a wonderful thing that he should be your substitute and stand in your room and place and stead, and bear your sin and all its curse and punishment, and that he should give his righteousness, yea, and his very self, to you that you might be saved. Ah, then you saw how sin could be overthrown, did you not? As soon as your heart understood Christ, then you saw that what the law could not do, in that it was weak through the flesh, Christ was able to accomplish, and that the power of sin and Satan under which you had been in bondage, and which you now loathed, could and would be broken and destroyed because Christ had come into the world to overcome it.

Next, do you recollect how you were led to see *the bruising of Christ's heel* and to stand in wonder and observe what the enmity of the serpent had wrought in him? Did you not begin to feel the bruised heel yourself? Did not sin torment you? Did not your own heart become a plague to you? Did not Satan begin to tempt you? Did he not inject blasphemous thoughts, and urge you on to desperate measures; did he not teach you to doubt the existence of God, and the mercy of God, and the possibility of your salvation, and so on? This was his nibbling at your heel. He is at his old tricks still. Did not your worldly friends begin to annoy you? Did they not give you the cold shoulder because they saw something about you so strange and foreign to their tastes? Did they not impute your conduct to fanaticism, pride, obstinacy, bigotry, and the like? Ah, this persecution is the serpent's seed beginning to discover the woman's seed, and carrying on the old war. What does Paul say? 'But as then he that was born after the flesh persecuted him that was born after the Spirit, even so it is now.' True godliness is an unnatural and strange thing to them, and they cannot away with it. Though there are no stakes in Smithfield, nor racks in the Tower, yet the enmity of the human heart towards Christ and his seed is just the same and very often shows itself in 'trials of cruel mockings' which to tender hearts are very hard to bear. Well, this is your heel being bruised in sympathy with the bruising of the heel of the glorious seed of the woman.

But, brethren, do you know something of the other fact, namely, that *we conquer, for the serpent's head is broken in us?* How, say you? Is not the power and dominion of sin broken in you? Do you not feel that you cannot sin because you are born of God? Some sins which were masters of you once, do not trouble you now. I have known a man guilty of profane swearing, and from the moment of his conversion he has never had any difficulty in the matter. We have known a man snatched from drunkenness, and the cure by divine grace has been very wonderful and complete. We have known persons delivered from unclean living, and they have at once become chaste and pure, because Christ has smitten the old dragon such blows that he could not have power over them in that respect. The chosen seed sin and mourn it, but they are not slaves to sin; their heart goeth not after it: they have to say sometimes, 'the thing I would not that I do,' but they are wretched when it is so. They consent with their heart to the law of God that it is good, and they sigh and cry that they may be helped to obey it, for they are no longer under the slavery of sin; the serpent's reigning power and dominion is broken in them.

It is broken next in this way, that the guilt of sin is gone. The great power of the serpent lies in unpardoned sin. He cries, 'I have made you guilty: I brought you under the curse.' 'No,' say we, 'we are delivered from the curse and are now blessed, for it is written, "Blessed is the man whose transgression is forgiven, and whose sin is covered." We are no longer guilty, for who shall lay anything to the charge of God's elect? Since Christ hath justified, who is he that condemneth?' Here is a swinging blow for the old dragon's head, such as he never will recover. Once in Christ we have no cause to fear the accuser of the brethren.

CONQUEROR OF SATAN

'Christ is our shield and hiding place!
  And shelter'd near his side.
We meet th'accuser face to face,
  And tell him "Jesus died."'

Oftentimes the Lord also grants us to know what it is to overcome temptation, and so to break the head of the fiend. Satan allures us with many baits; he has studied our points well, he knows the weakness of the flesh: but many and many a time, blessed be God, we have foiled him completely to his eternal shame! The devil must have felt himself mean that day when he tried to overthrow Job, dragged him down to a dunghill, robbed him of everything, covered him with sores, and yet could not make him yield. Job conquered when he cried, 'Though he slay me yet will I trust in him.' A feeble man had vanquished a devil who could raise the wind and blow down a house, and destroy the family who were feasting in it. Devil as he is, and crowned prince of the power of the air, yet the poor bereaved patriarch sitting on the dunghill covered with sores, being one of the woman's seed, through the strength of the inner life won the victory over him.

'Ye sons of God oppose his rage,
  Resist and he'll be gone:
Thus did our dearest Lord engage
  And vanquish him alone.

Moreover, dear brethren, we have this hope that the very being of sin in us will be destroyed. The day will come when we shall be without spot or wrinkle, or any such thing; and we shall stand before the throne of God, having suffered no injury whatever from the fall and from all the machinations of Satan, for 'they are without fault before the throne of God.' What triumph that will be! 'The Lord will tread Satan under your feet shortly.' When he has made you perfect and free from all sin, as he will do, you will have bruised the serpent's head indeed.

And your resurrection, too, when Satan shall see you come up from the grave like one that has been perfumed in a bath of spices, when he shall see you arise in the image of Christ, with the same body which was sown in corruption and weakness raised in incorruption and power, then will he feel an infinite chagrin, and know that his head is bruised by the woman's seed.

I ought to add that every time any one of us is made useful in saving souls we do, as it were, repeat the bruising of the serpent's head. When you go, dear sister, among those poor children, and pick them up from the gutters, where they are Satan's prey, where he finds the raw material for thieves and criminals, and when through your means, by the grace of God, the little wanderers become children of the living God, then you in your measure bruise the old serpent's head. I pray you do not spare him. When we by preaching the gospel turn sinners from the error of their ways, so that they escape from the power of darkness, again we bruise the serpent's head. Whenever in any shape or way you are blessed to the aiding of the cause of truth and righteousness in the world, you too, who were once beneath his power, and even now have sometimes to suffer from his nibbling at your heel, you tread upon his head. In all deliverances and victories, you overcome, and prove the promise true, – 'Thou shalt tread upon the lion and adder: the young lion and the dragon shalt thou trample under feet. Because he hath set his love upon me, therefore will I deliver him: I will set him on high, because he hath known my name.'

3. Let us speak awhile upon THE ENCOURAGE-
MENT which our text and the context yields to us; for
it seems to me to abound.

I want you, brethren, to exercise faith in the promise and be comforted. The text evidently encouraged
Adam very much. I do not think we have attached
enough importance to the conduct of Adam after the
Lord had spoken to him. Notice the simple but con-
clusive proof which he gave of his faith. Sometimes an
action may be very small and unimportant, and yet, as
a straw shows which way the wind blows, it may
display at once, if it be thought over, the whole state
of the man's mind. Adam acted in faith upon what
God said, for we read, 'And Adam called his wife's
name Eve (or Life); because she was the mother of all
living' (verse 20). She was not a mother at all, but as
the life was to come through her by virtue of the
promised seed, Adam marks his full conviction of the
truth of the promise though at the time the woman
had borne no children. There stood Adam, fresh from
the awful presence of God, what more could he say?
He might have said with the prophet, 'My flesh
trembleth for the fear of thee,' but even then he turns
round to his fellow culprit as she stands there trembling too, and he calls her Eve, mother of the life that is
yet to be. It was grandly spoken by Father Adam: it
makes him rise in our esteem. Had he been left to
himself he would have murmured or at least de-
spaired, but no, his faith in the new promise gave him
hope. He uttered no word of repining against the
condemnation to till with toil the unthankful ground,
nor on Eve's part was there a word of repining over
the appointed sorrows of motherhood; they each
accept the well-deserved sentence with the silence
which denotes the perfection of their resignation; their
only word is full of simple faith. There was no child on

whom to set their hopes, nor would the true seed be born for many an age, still Eve is to be the mother of all living, and he calls her so. Exercise like faith, my brother, on the far wider revelation which God has given to you, and always extract the utmost comfort from it. Make a point, whenever you receive a promise from God, to get all you can out of it: if you carry out that rule, it is wonderful what comfort you will gain. Some go on the principle of getting as little as possible out of God's word. Such a plan may be wise with a man's word; but God's word is to be understood at the maximum, for he will do exceeding abundantly above what you ask or even think.

Notice, by way of further encouragement, that we may regard our reception of Christ's righteousness as an instalment of the final overthrow of the devil. The twenty-first verse says, 'Unto Adam also and to his wife did the Lord God make coats of skins, and clothed them.' A very condescending, thoughtful, and instructive deed of divine love! God heard what Adam said to his wife, and saw that he was a believer, and so he comes and gives him the type of the perfect righteousness, which is the believer's portion – he covered him with lasting raiment. No more fig leaves which were a mere mockery, but a close fitting garment which had been procured through the death of a victim; the Lord brings that and puts it on him and Adam could no more say, 'I am naked.' How could he, for God had clothed him. Now, beloved, let us take out of the promise that is given us concerning our Lord's conquest over the devil this one item and rejoice in it, for Christ has delivered us from the power of the serpent, who opened our eyes and told us we were naked, by covering us from head to foot with a righteousness which adorns and protects us, so that we are comfortable in heart, and beautiful in the sight of God, and are no more ashamed.

Next, by way of encouragement in pursuing the Christian life, I would say to young people, expect to be assailed. If you have fallen into trouble through being a Christian, be encouraged by it; do not at all regret or fear it, but rejoice ye in that day, and leap for joy, for this is the constant token of the covenant. There is enmity between the seed of the woman and the seed of the serpent still, and if you did not experience any of it you might begin to fear that you were on the wrong side. Now that you smart under the sneer of sarcasm and oppression, rejoice and triumph, for now are ye partakers with the glorious seed of the woman in the bruising of his heel.

Still further encouragement comes from this. Your suffering as Christians is not brought upon you for your own sake; ye are partners with the great seed of the woman, ye are confederates with Christ. You must not think the devil cares much about you: the battle is against Christ in you. When you were without Christ in the world you might have sinned as you like, your relatives and workmates would not have been at all grieved with you, they would rather have joined you in it; but now the serpent's seed hates Christ in you. This exalts the sufferings of persecution to a position far above all common afflictions. I have heard of a woman who was condemned to death in the Marian days, and before her time came to be burned a child was born to her, and she cried out in her sorrow. A wicked adversary, who stood by said, 'How will you bear to die for your religion if you make such ado?' 'Ah,' she said, 'now I suffer in my own person as a woman, but then *I* shall not suffer, but Christ in me.' Nor were these idle words, for she bore her martyrdom with exemplary patience, and rose in her chariot of fire in holy triumph to heaven. If Christ be in you, nothing will dismay you, but you will overcome the world, the flesh and the devil by faith.

Last of all, let us resist the devil always with this belief, that he has received a broken head. I am inclined to think that Luther's way of laughing at the devil was a very good one, for he is worthy of shame and everlasting contempt. Luther once threw an inkstand at his head when he was tempting him very sorely, and though the act itself appears absurd enough, yet it was a true type of what that greatest Reformer was doing all his life long, for the books he wrote were truly a flinging of the inkstand at the head of the fiend. That is what we have to do: we are to resist him by all means. Let us do this bravely, and tell him to his teeth that we are not afraid of him. Tell him to recollect his bruised head, which he tries to cover with a crown of pride, or with a popish cowl, or with an infidel doctor's hood. We know him and see the deadly wound he bears. His power is gone; he is fighting a lost battle; he is contending against omnipotence. He has set himself against the oath of the Father; against the blood of the incarnate Son; against the eternal power and Godhead of the blessed Spirit, all of which are engaged in the defence of the seed of the woman in the day of battle. Therefore, brethren, be ye steadfast in resisting the evil one, being strong in faith, giving glory to God.

> ''Tis by thy blood, immortal Lamb,
>   Thine armies tread the tempter down;
> 'Tis by thy word and powerful name
>   They gain the battle and renown.
>
> 'Rejoice ye heavens; let every star
>   Shine with new glories round the sky:
> Saints, while ye sing the heavenly war,
>   Raise your Deliverer's name on high.'

CHRIST
THE OVERCOMER OF
THE WORLD

'Be of good cheer; I have overcome the world.'
– John 16:33

When these words were spoken our Saviour was about to leave his disciples to go to his death for their sakes. His great anxiety was that they might not be too much cast down by the trials which would come upon them. He desired to prepare their minds for the heavy sorrows which awaited them, while the powers of darkness and the men of the world wrought their will upon him. Now observe, that our Lord Jesus, in whom dwells infinite wisdom, knew all the secret springs of comfort, and all the hallowed sources of consolation in heaven and under heaven, and yet in order to console his disciples he spoke, not of heavenly mysteries nor of secrets hidden in the breast of God, but he spake concerning himself. Doth he not herein teach us that there is no balm for the heart like himself, no consolation of Israel comparable to his person and his work. If even such a divine Barnabas, such a firstborn son of consolation as the Lord himself must point to what he himself has done, for only so can he make his followers to be of good cheer, then how wise it must be in ministers to preach much of Jesus by way of encouragement to the Lord's afflicted, and how prudent it is for mourners to look to him for the comfort they need. 'Be of good cheer,' he saith, *'I'* – something about himself – *'I have* overcome the world.' So then, beloved, in all times of depression of spirit hasten away to the Lord Jesus Christ; whenever the cares of this life burden you, and your way seems hard for your weary feet, fly to your Lord. There may be, and there are, other sources of consolation, but they will not at all times serve your turn; but in him there dwelleth such a fulness of comfort, that whether it be in summer or in winter the streams of comfort are always flowing. In your high state or in your low estate, and from whatever quarter your trouble may arise, you can resort at once to him and you shall find that he strengthens the hands that hang down and confirms the feeble knees.

A further remark suggests itself that the Lord Jesus must be more than man from the tone which he assumed. There are certain persons who deny the Godhead of our Lord and yet think well of Jesus as a man; indeed, they have uttered many highly complimentary things with regard to his character: but I wonder it should not strike them that there is a great deal of assumption, presumption, pride, egotism, and all that style of folly in this man if he be nothing more than a man. For what good man whom you would wish to imitate would say to others, 'Be of good cheer; I have overcome the world.' This is altogether too much for a mere man to say. The Lord Jesus Christ frequently spoke about himself and about what he had done, and commended himself to his disciples as one who was only a man and of a lowly mind could never have done. The Lord was certainly meek and lowly in heart, but no man of that character would have told others so. There is an inconsistency here which none can account for but those who believe him to be the Son of God. Understand him to be divine, put him in his true position as speaking down out of the excellency of his deity to his disciples, and then you can comprehend his so speaking, yea, it becomes infinitely seemly and beautiful. Deny his Godhead, and I for one am quite unable to understand how the words before us, and others like them, could ever have fallen from his lips, for none will dare to say that he was boastful. Blessed be thou, O Son of man, thou art also Son of God, and therefore thou dost not only speak to us with the sympathizing tenderness of a brother man, but with the majestic authority of the Only Begotten of the Father. Divinely condescending are the words, 'I have overcome the world.'

If you look at this claim of Jesus without the eye of faith, does it not wear an extraordinary appearance? How could the betrayed man of Nazareth say, 'I have overcome the world?' We can imagine Napoleon speaking thus when he had crushed the nations beneath his feet, and shaped the map of Europe to his will. We can imagine Alexander speaking thus when he had rifled the palaces of Persia and led her ancient monarchs captive. But who is this that speaketh on this wise? It is a Galilean, who wears a peasant's garment, and consorts with the poor and the fallen! He has neither wealth nor worldly rank nor honour among men, and yet speaks of having overcome the world. He is about to be betrayed by his own base follower into the hands of his enemies, and then he will be led out to judgment and to death, and yet he says, 'I have overcome the world.' He is casting an eye to his cross with all its shame, and to the death which ensued from it, and yet he saith, 'I have overcome the world.' He had nowhere to lay his head, he had not a disciple that would stand up for him, for he had just said, 'Ye shall be scattered, every man to his own, and shall leave me alone;' he was to be charged with blasphemy and sedition, and brought before the judge, and find no man to declare his generation; he was to be given up to a brutal soldiery to be mocked and despitefully used and spat upon; his hands and feet were to be nailed to a cross, that he might die a felon's death, and yet he saith, 'I have overcome the world.' How marvellous, and yet how true! He spoke not after the manner of the flesh nor after the sight of the eye. We must use faith's optics here and look within the veil, and then we shall see not alone the despised bodily person of the Son of man, but the indwelling, noble, all-conquering soul which transformed shame into honour, and death into glory. May God the Holy Spirit enable us to look through the external to the internal, and see how marvellously the ignominious death was the rough garment which concealed the matchless victory from the purblind eyes of carnal man.

In the preceding sermons I have spoken of our Lord Jesus Christ: first, as the End of the Law; and secondly, as the Conqueror over the old serpent; now we come to speak of him as *the overcomer of the world.* Addressing his disciples he said, 'Be of good cheer; I have overcome the world.'

Now, *what is this world that he speaks about?* and *how has he overcome it?* and *what good cheer is there in the fact for us?*

1. WHAT IS THIS WORLD WHICH HE IS RE-FERRING TO? I scarcely know a word which is used with so many senses as this word 'world.' If you will turn to your Bibles you will find the word 'world' used in significations widely different, for there is a world which Christ made, 'He was in the world and the world was made by him' – that is, the physical world. There is a world which God so loved that he gave his only begotten Son that whosoever believeth in him might not perish. There are several forms of this favourable signification. Then there is a world, the world here meant, which 'lieth in the wicked one,' a world which knows not Christ, but which is evermore opposed to him: a world for which he says that he does

not pray, and a world which he would not have us love – 'Love not the world, neither the things which are in the world.' Without going into these various meanings, and shades of meaning, which are very abundant, let us just say that we scarcely know how to define what is meant here in so many words, though we know well enough what is meant. Scripture does not give us definitions, but uses language in a popular manner, since it speaks to common people. 'The world' is very much the equivalent of the 'seed of the serpent,' of which we spoke in the previous sermon. The world here means the visible embodiment of that spirit of evil which was in the serpent, and which now worketh in the children of disobedience; it is the human form of the same evil force with which our Lord contended when he overcame the devil; it means the power of evil in the unregenerate mass of mankind, the energy and power of sin as it dwells in that portion of the world which abideth in death and lieth in the wicked one. The devil is the god of this world, and the prince of this world, and therefore he who is the friend of this world is the enemy of God. The world is the opposite of the church. There is a church which Christ has redeemed and chosen out of the world and separated unto himself, from among men, and of these as renewed by the power of divine grace, he says, 'Ye are not of the world, even as I am not of the world,' and again, 'Because ye are not of the world, but I have chosen you out of the world, therefore the world hateth you.' Now, the rest of mankind not comprehended amongst the chosen, the redeemed, the called, the saved, are called the world. Of these our Lord said, 'O righteous Father, the world hath not known thee;' and John said, 'The world knoweth us not because it knew him not.' This is the power which displays a deadly enmity against Christ and against his chosen; hence it is called 'this present evil world,' while the kingdom of grace is spoken of as 'the world to come.' This is the world of which it is said, 'He that is born of God overcometh the world.'

You will see that 'the world' includes the ungodly themselves, as well as the force of evil in them, but it marks them out, not as creatures nor even as men who have sinned, but as unregenerate, carnal and rebellious, and therefore as the living embodiments of an evil power which works against God; and so we read of 'the world of the ungodly.'

Perhaps I ought to add that there has grown up out of the existence of unconverted men and the prevalence of sin in them, certain customs, fashions, maxims, rules, modes, manners, forces, all of which go to make up what is called 'the world,' and there are also certain principles, desires, lusts, governments and powers which also make up a part of the evil thing called 'the world.' Jesus says, 'My kingdom is not of this world.' James speaks of keeping ourselves 'unspotted from the world.' John says, 'The world passeth away and the lust thereof;' and Paul says, 'Be not conformed to this world, but be ye transformed.'

Moreover, I may say that the present constitution and arrangement of all things in this fallen state may be comprehended in the term 'world,' for everything has come under vanity by reason of sin, and things are not today according to the original plan of the Most High, as designed for man in his innocence. Behold, there are trials and troubles springing out of our very existence in this life of which it is said, 'in the world ye shall have tribulation.' To many a child of God there have befallen hunger and disease and suffering, and unkindness, and various forms of evil which belong not to the world to come, nor to the kingdom which Christ has set up, but which come to them because they are in this present evil world, which has so become because the race of men have fallen under the curse and consequence of sin.

Now the world is all these matters put together, this great conglomeration of mischief among men, this evil which dwelleth here and there and everywhere wherever men are scattered – this is the thing which we call the world. Every one of us knows better what it is than he can tell to anybody else, and perhaps while I am explaining I am rather confounding than expounding. You know just what the world is to some of you – it is not more than your own little family, as to outward form, but much more as to influence. Your actual world may be confined to your own house, but the same principles enter into the domestic circle which pervade kingdoms and states. To others the world takes a wide sweep as they necessarily meet with ungodly men in business, and this we must do unless we are to go altogether out of the world, which is no part of our Lord's plan, for he says, 'I pray not that thou shouldest take them out of the world.' To some who look at the whole mass of mankind, and are called thoughtfully to consider them all, because they have to be God's messengers to them, the tendencies and outgoings of the human mind towards that which is evil, and the spirit of men's actions as done against God in all nations and ages – all these go to make up to them 'the world.' But be it what it may, it is a thing out of which tribulation will be sure to come to us, Christ tells us so. It may come in the form of temporal trial of some shape or other; it may come in the form of temptation which will alight upon us from our fellow men; it may come in the form of persecution to a greater or less extent according to our position: but it will come. 'In the world ye shall have tribulation.' We are sojourners in an enemy's country, and the people of the land wherein we tarry are not our friends, and will not help us on our pilgrimage to heaven. All spiritual men in the world are our friends, but then, like ourselves, they are in the world but they are not of it. From the kingdom of this world whereof Satan is lord we must expect fierce opposition, against which we must contend even unto victory if we are to enter into everlasting rest.

2. Now this brings me, in the second place, to the more interesting topic of HOW HAS CHRIST OVERCOME THE WORLD? And we answer, first, he did so *in his life:* then *in his death:* and then *in his rising and his reigning.*

First, Christ *overcame the world in his life.* This is a wonderful study, the overcoming of the world in the life of Christ. I reckon that those first thirty years of which we know so little were a wonderful preparation for this conflict with the world, and that though only in the carpenter's shop, and obscure, and unknown to the great outside world, yet in fact he was not merely preparing for the battle, but he was then beginning to overcome it. In the patience which made him bide his time we see the dawn of the victory. When we are intent upon doing good, and we see mischief and sin triumphant everywhere, we are eager to begin: but suppose it were not the great Father's will that we should be immediately engaged in the fray, how strongly would the world then tempt us to go forward before our time. A transgression of discipline may be caused by over zeal, and this as much breaks through the law of obedience as dulness or sloth would do. The Roman soldier was accounted guilty who, when the army was left with the orders that no man should strike a blow in the leader's absence, nevertheless stepped forward and slew a Gaul; the act was one of valour but it was contrary to military discipline, and might have had most baleful results, and so it was condemned. Thus is it sometimes with us; before we are ready, before we have received our commission, we are in haste to step foward and smite the foe. That temptation must have come to Christ from the world: many a time as he heard of what was going on in the reign of error and hypocrisy his benevolent impulses might have suggested to him to be up and doing, had it not been that he was incapable of wrong desires. Doubtless he was willing to be healing the sick. Was not the land full of sufferers? He would fain be saving souls – were they not going down to the pit by thousands? He would gladly have confuted error, for falsehood was doing deadly work, but his hour was not yet come. Yet our Lord and Master had nothing to say till his Father bade him speak. Strongly under an impulse to be at work we know he was, for when he went up to the temple he said, 'Wist ye not that I must be about my Father's business?' That utterance revealed the fire that burned within his soul, and yet he was not preaching, nor healing, nor disputing, but still remained in obscurity all those thirty years, because God would have it so. When the Lord would have us quiet we are doing his will best by being quiet, but yet to be still and calm for so long a time was a wonderful instance of how all his surroundings could not master him, not even when they seemed to work with his philanthropy; he still remained obedient to God, and thus proved himself the overcomer of the world.

When he appears upon the scene of public action you know how he overcomes the world in many ways. First, *by remaining always faithful to his testimony.* He never modified it, not even by so much as a solitary word to please the sons of men. From the first day in which he began to preach even to the closing sentence which he uttered, it was all truth and nothing but truth, truth uncoloured by prevailing sentiment, untainted by popular error. He did not, after the manner of the Jesuit, disguise his doctrine by so shaping it that men would hardly know but what it was the very error in which they had been brought up, but he came out with plain speaking, and set himself in opposition to all the powers which ruled the thought and creed of the age. He was no guarder of truth. He allowed truth to fight her own battles in her own way, and you know how she bares her breast to her antagonist's darts, and finds in her own immutable, immortal, and invulnerable life her shield and her spear. His speech was confident, for he knew that truth would conquer in the long run, and therefore he gave forth his doctrine without respect to the age or its prejudices. I do not think that you say that of anybody else's ministry, not even of the best and bravest of his servants. We can see, in looking at Luther, great and glorious Luther, how Romanism tinged all that he did more or less; and the darkness of the age cast some gloom even over the serene and steadfast soul of Calvin; of each one of the Reformers we must say the same: bright stars as all of these were, yet they kept not themselves untarnished by the sphere in which they shone. Every man is more or less affected by his age, and we are obliged, as we read history, to make continual allowances, for we all admit that it would not be fair to judge the men of former times by the standard of the nineteenth century. But, beloved, you may test Christ Jesus if you will by the nineteenth century light, if light it be; you may judge him by any century, ay, you may try him by the bright light of the throne of God: his teaching is pure truth without any admixture, it will stand the test of time and of eternity. His teaching was not affected by the fact of his being born a Jew, nor by the prevalence of the Rabbinical traditions, nor by the growth of the Greek philosophy, nor by any other of the peculiar influences which were then abroad. His teaching was in the world, but it was not of it, nor tinged by it. It was the truth as he had received it from the Father, and the world could not make him add to it, or take from it, or change it in the least degree, and therefore in this respect he overcame the world.

Observe him, next, in *the deep calm which pervaded his spirit at times when he received the approbation of men*. Our Lord was popular to a very high degree at certain times. How the people thronged around him as his benevolent hands scattered healing on all sides. How they approved of him when he fed them; but how clearly he saw through that selfish approbation, and said, 'Ye seek me because of the loaves and the fishes.' He never lost his self-possession: you never find him elated by the multitudes following him. There is not an expression that he ever used which even contains a suspicion of self-glorification. Amid their hosannahs his mind is quietly reposing in God. He leaves their acclamations and applause to refresh himself by prayer upon the cold mountains, in the midnight air. He communed with God, and so lived above the praises of men. He walked among them, holy, harmless, undefiled and separate from sinners, even when they would have taken him by force and made him a king. Once he rides in triumph, as he might often have done if he had pleased, but then it was in such humble style that his pomp was far other than that of kings, a manifestation of lowliness rather than a display of majesty. Amid the willing hosannas of little children, and of those whom he had blessed he rides along, but you can see that he indulges none of the thoughts of a worldly conqueror, none of the proud ideas of the warrior who returns from the battle stained with blood. No, he is still as meek and as gentle and as kindly as ever he was, and his triumph has not a grain of self-exaltation in it. He had overcome the world. What could the world give him, brethren? An imperial nature like to his, in which the manhood held such close communion with Deity as is not readily to be imagined, what was there here below to cause pride in him? If the trump of fame had sounded out its loudest note, what could it have been compared with the songs of cherubim and seraphim to which his ear had been accustomed throughout all ages? No, allied with his deity, his manhood was superior to all the arts of flattery, and to all the honours which mankind could offer him. He overcame the world.

He was the same when the world tried the other plan upon him. *It frowned at him, but he was calm still.* He had scarcely commenced to preach before they would have cast him from the brow of the hill headlong. Do you not expect, as they are hurrying him to the precipice, to see him turn round upon them and denounce them at least with burning words, such as Elias used? But no, he speaks not an angry word; he passes away and is gone out of their midst. In the synagogue they often gnashed their teeth upon him in their malice, but if ever he was moved to indignation it was not because of anything directed against himself; he always bore all, and scarcely ever spoke a word by way of reply to merely personal attacks. If calumnies were heaped upon him he went on as calmly as if they had not abused him, nor desired to slay him. When he is brought before his judges what a difference there is between the Master and his servant Paul. He is smitten, but he does not say like Paul, 'God shall smite thee, thou whited wall;' no, but like a lamb before her shearers he is dumb and openeth not his mouth. If they could have made him angry they would have overcome him; but he was loving still; he was gentle, quiet, patient, however much they provoked him. Point me to an impatient word – there is not even a tradition of an angry look that he gave on account of any offence rendered to himself. They could not drive him from his purposes of love, nor could they make him say anything or do anything that was contrary to perfect love. He calls down no fire from heaven: no she-bears come out of the wood to devour those who have mocked him. No, he can say, 'I have overcome the world,' for whether it smile or whether it frown, in the perfect peace and quiet of his spirit, in the delicious calm of communion with God, the Man of Sorrows holds on his conquering way.

His victory will be seen in another form. He overcame the world as to *the unselfishness of his aims*. When men find themselves in a world like this they generally say, 'What is our market? What can we make out of it?' This is how they are trained from childhood. 'Boy, you have to fight your own way, mind you look to your own interests and rise in the world.' The book which is commended to the young man shows him how to make the best use of all things for himself, he must take care of 'number one,' and mind the main chance. The boy is told by his wise instructors, 'You must look to yourself or nobody else will look to you: and whatever you may do for others, be doubly sure to guard your own interests.' That is the world's prudence, the essence of all her politics, the basis of her political economy – every man, and every nation must take care of themselves: if you wish for any other politics or economics you will be considered to be foolish theorists and probably a little touched in the head. Self is the man, the world's law of self-preservation is the sovereign rule, and nothing can go on rightly if you interfere with the gospel of selfishness; so the commercial and political Solomons assure us. Now, look at the Lord Jesus Christ when he was in the world and you will learn nothing of such principles, except their condemnation: the world could not overcome him by leading him into a selfish mode of action. Did it ever enter into his soul, even for a moment, what he could do for himself? There were riches but he had not where to lay his head. The little store he had he committed to the trust of Judas, and as long as there were any poor in the land they were sure to share in what was in the bag. He set so little account by estate, and goods, and lands, that no mention is made of such things by either of his four biographers. He had wholly and altogether risen above the world in that respect; for with whatever evil the most spiteful infidels have ever charged our Lord, they have never, to my knowledge, accused him of avarice, greed, or selfishness in any form. He had overcome the world.

Then again the Master overcame the world, in that *he did not stoop to use its power.* He did not use that form of power which is peculiar to the world even for unselfish purposes. I can conceive a man, even apart from the Spirit of God, rising superior to riches, and desiring only the promotion of some great principle which has possessed his heart; but you will usually notice that when men have done so, they have been ready to promote good by evil, or at least they have judged that great principles might be pushed on by force of arms, or bribes, or policy. Mahomet had grasped a grand truth when he said, 'There is no god but God.' The unity of the Godhead is a truth of the utmost value; but then here comes the means to be used for the propagation of this grand truth – the scimitar. 'Off with the infidels' heads! If they have false gods, or will not own the unity of the Godhead, they are not fit to live.' Can you imagine our Lord

Jesus Christ doing this? Why then the world would have conquered him. But he conquered the world in that he would not employ in the slightest degree this form of power. He might have gathered a troop about him, and his heroic example, together with his miraculous power, must soon have swept away the Roman empire, and converted the Jew; and then across Europe and Asia and Africa his victorious legions might have gone trampling down all manner of evil, and with the cross for his banner and the sword for his weapon, the idols would have fallen, and the whole world must have been made to bow at his feet. But no, when Peter takes out the sword, he says, 'Put up thy sword into its sheath, they that take the sword shall perish with the sword.' Well did he say, 'My kingdom is not of this world, else would my servants fight.'

And he might if he had pleased have allied his church with the state, as his mistaken friends have done in these degenerate times, and then there might have been penal laws against those who dared dissent, and there might have been forced contributions for the support of his church and such like things. You have read, I dare say, of such things being done, but not in the Gospels, nor in the Acts of the Apostles. These things are done by those who forget the Christ of God, for he uses no instrument but love, no sword but the truth, no power but the Eternal Spirit, and, in the very fact that he put all the worldly forces aside, he overcame the world.

So, brethren, he overcame the world by *his fearlessness of the world's élite,* for many a man who has braved the frowns of the multitude cannot bear the criticism of the few who think they have monopolized all wisdom. But Christ meets the Pharisee, and pays no honour to his phylactery; he confronts the Sadducee, and yields not to his cold philosophy, neither does he conceal the difficulties of the faith to escape his sneer; and he braves also the Herodian, who is the worldly politician, and he gives him an un-answerable reply. He is the same before them all, master in all positions, overcoming the world's wisdom and supposed intelligence by his own simple testimony to the truth.

And he overcame the world in his life best of all *by the constancy of his love.* He loved the most unlovely men, he loved those who hated him, he loved those who despised him. You and I are readily turned aside from loving when we receive ungrateful treatment, and thus we are conquered by the world; but he kept to his great object – 'He saved others, himself he could not save;' and he died with this prayer on his lips, 'Father, forgive them, for they know not what they do.' Not soured in the least, thou blessed Saviour, thou art at the last just as tender as at the first. We have seen fine spirits, full of generosity, who have had to deal with a crooked and perverse generation, until they have at last grown hard and cold. Nero, who weeps when he signs the first death warrant of a criminal, at last comes to gloat in the blood of his subjects. Thus do sweet flowers wither into noxious corruption. As for thee, thou precious Saviour, thou art ever fragrant with love. No spot comes upon thy lovely character, though thou dost traverse a miry road. Thou art as kind to men at thy departure as thou wast at thy coming, for thou hast overcome the world.

I can only say on the next point that *Christ by his death overcame the world* because, by a wondrous act of self-sacrifice, the Son of God smote to the heart the principle of selfishness, which is the very soul and life-blood of the world. There, too, by redeeming fallen man he lifted man up from the power which the world exercises over him, for he taught men that they are redeemed, that they are no longer their own but bought with a price, and thus redemption became the note of liberty from the bondage of self-love, and the hammer which breaks the fetters of the world and the lusts thereof.

By reconciling men unto God through his great atonement, he has also removed them from the despair which else had kept them down in sin, and made them the willing slaves of the world. Now are they pardoned, and, being justified, they are made to be the friends of God, and being the friends of God they become enemies to God's enemies, and are separated from the world, and so the world by Christ's death is overcome.

But chiefly has he overcome *by his rising and his reigning,* for when he rose he bruised the serpent's head, and that serpent is the prince of this world, and hath dominion over it. Christ has conquered the world's prince and led him in chains, and now hath Christ assumed the sovereignty over all things here below. God hath put all things under his feet. At his girdle are the keys of providence; he ruleth amongst the multitude and in the council chambers of kings. As Joseph governed Egypt for the good of Israel, so doth Jehovah Jesus govern all things for the good of his people. Now the world can go no further in persecuting his people than he permits it. Not a martyr can burn, nor a confessor be imprisoned without the permit of Jesus Christ who is the Lord of all; for the government is upon his shoulders and his kingdom ruleth over all. Brethren, this is a great joy to us to think of the reigning power of Christ as having overcome the world.

There is yet this other thought, that he has overcome the world *by the gift of the Holy Spirit.* That gift was practically the world's conquest. Jesus has set up a rival kingdom now: a kingdom of love and righteousness; already the world feels its power by the Spirit. I do not believe that there is a dark place in the centre of Africa which is not to some extent improved by the influence of Christianity; even the wilderness rejoices and is glad for him. No barbarous power dares to do what once it did, or, if it does, there is such a clamour raised against its cruelty that very soon it has to say *peccavi*, and confess its faults. This moment the stone cut out of the mountain without hands has begun to smite old Dagon, it is breaking his head and breaking his hands and the very stump of him shall be dashed in pieces yet. There is no power in this world so vital, so potent as the power of Christ at this day. I say naught just now of heavenly or spiritual things; but I speak only of temporal and moral influences – even in these the cross is to the front. He of whom Voltaire said that he lived in the twilight of his day, is going from strength to strength. It was true it was the twilight, but it was the twilight of the morning, and the full noon is coming. Every year the name of Jesus brings more light to this poor world; every year hastens on the time when the cross which is the Pharos of humanity, the world's lighthouse amid the storm, shall shine forth more and more brightly over the troubled waters till the great calm shall come. The word shall become more and more universally true, 'I, if I be lifted up, will draw all men unto me.' Thus hath he overcome the world.

3. Now, lastly, WHAT CHEER IS THERE HERE FOR US? Why, this first, that if the man Christ Jesus has overcome the world at its worst, we who are in him shall overcome the world too through the same power which dwelt in him. He has put his life into his people, he has given his Spirit to dwell in them, and

they shall be more than conquerors. He overcame the world when it attacked him in the worst possible shape, for he was poorer than any of his people, he was more sick and sad than any of them, he was more despised and persecuted than any of his saints are at this present time, and he was deprived of certain divine consolations which God has promised never to take away from them, and yet with all possible disadvantages Christ overcame the world: therefore be assured we shall conquer also by his strength. Besides, he overcame the world when nobody else had overcome it. It was as it were a young lion which had never been defeated in fight: it roared upon him out of the thicket and leaped upon him in the fulness of its strength. Now if our greater Samson did tear this young lion as though it were a kid and fling it down as a vanquished thing, you may depend upon it that now it is an old lion, and grey and covered with the wounds which he gave it of old, we, having the Lord's life and power in us, will overcome it too. Blessed be his name! What good cheer there is in his victory. He does as good as say to us, 'I have overcome the world, and you in whom I dwell, who are clothed with my spirit, must overcome it too.'

But then, next, remember he overcame the world as our Head and representative, and it may truly be said that if the members do not overcome, then the head has not perfectly gained the victory. If it were possible for the members to be defeated, why then, the head itself could not claim a complete victory, since it is one with the members. So Jesus Christ, our covenant Head and representative, in whose loins lay all the spiritual seed, conquered the world for us and we conquered the world in him. He is our Adam, and what was done by him was actually done for us and virtually done by us. Have courage then, for you must conquer; it must happen to you as unto your head: where the head is shall the members be, and as the head is so must the members be: wherefore be assured of the palm branch and the crown.

And now, brethren, I ask you whether you have not found it so? Is it not true at this moment that the world is overcome in you? Does self govern you? Are you working to acquire wealth for your own aggrandisement? Are you living to win honour and fame among men? Are you afraid of men's frowns? Are you the slave of popular opinion? Do you do things because it is the custom to do them? Are you the slave of fashion? If you are, you know nothing about this victory. But if you are a true Christian I know what you can say: 'Lord, I am thy servant, thou has loosed my bonds; henceforth the world hath no dominion over me; and though it tempt me, and frighten me, and flatter me, yet still I rise superior to it by the power of thy Spirit, for the love of Christ constraineth me, and I live not unto myself and unto things that are seen, but unto Christ and to things invisible.' If it be so, who has done this for you? Who but Christ the Overcomer, who is formed in you the hope of glory: wherefore be of good cheer, for you have overcome the world by virtue of his dwelling in you.

So, brethren, let us go back to the world and its tribulations without fear. Its trials cannot hurt us. In the process we shall get good, as the wheat doth out of the threshing. Let us go forth to combat the world, for it cannot overcome us. There was never a man yet with the life of God in his soul whom the whole world could subdue; nay, all the world and hell together cannot conquer the veriest babe in the family of the Lord Jesus Christ. Lo, ye are harnessed with salvation, ye are panoplied with omnipotence, your heads are covered with the aegis of the atonement, and Christ himself, the Son of God, is your captain. Take up your battle cry with courage, and fear not, for more is he that is for you than all they that be against you. It is said of the glorified saints, 'They overcame through the blood of the Lamb;' 'and this is the victory that overcometh the world, even our faith,' wherefore be ye steadfast, even to the end, for ye shall be more than conquerors through him that hath loved you. Amen.

CHRIST
THE MAKER OF ALL
THINGS NEW

'Therefore if any man be in Christ, he is a new creature: old things are passed away; behold, all things are become new.' – 2 Corinthians 5:17

We shall now try to set forth our Lord Jesus Christ as the Author of the New Creation, and may we be enabled by the Holy Spirit to speak to his glory. To create all things new is one of his most famous achievements; may we not only gaze upon it but be partakers in it.

What says Solomon in the Book of Ecclesiastes? Does he not tell us there that 'the thing that hath been shall be, and that which is done is that which shall be done, and there is no new thing under the sun'? No doubt Solomon was correct in this declaration, but he wrote of this world and not of the world to come whereof we speak; for behold, in the world to come, that is to say, in the kingdom of our Lord Jesus Christ, all things are new. To the wisest mind, if unrenewed, there is nothing new, but to the humblest of the regenerated ones all things have become new.

The word 'new' seems to harmonize sweetly with the name and work of our Lord Jesus, inasmuch as he comes in after the old system had failed, and begins anew with us as the father and head of a chosen race. He is the Mediator of the new covenant, and has come to place us in a new relationship towards God. As the second Adam he has delivered us from the old broken covenant of works wherein we lay under the curse, and he hath placed us under the new infallible covenant of grace wherein we are established by his merit. The blood of Jesus Christ is said to be 'the blood of the new covenant;' there is thus a connection with newness even in the most vital point of our dear Redeemer's person. The blood is even to him the life thereof, and apart from that blood he can bestow no remission of sin; thus there is a newness about that *essential life-blood,* for when he gives us to drink of his cup of remembrance he says, 'This is my blood of the *new* testament, which is shed for many for the remission of sins.' 'Now hath he obtained a more excellent ministry, by how much also he is the Mediator of a better covenant, which was established upon better promises.' The old covenant, the old ceremonial law, the old spirit of bondage, and the whole of the old leaven Jesus has purged out of the house, and he has admitted to a new dispensation wherein grace reigns through righteousness unto eternal life.

When our Lord Jesus came into the world his birth of a virgin by the power of the Holy Ghost was a new thing, for thus had the prophet Jeremiah said of old in the name of the Lord, 'How long wilt thou go about, O thou backsliding daughter? For the Lord hath created a new thing in the earth, a woman shall compass a man.' Unto us a child is born who is the virgin's son, in whom we do rejoice because he cometh into the world without taint of original sin, after a new fashion, as never man was born before. Coming thus into the old world, he publisheth new doctrine, for his doctrine is called gospel, or good news. It is the freshest news that an anxious heart can hear; it is the most novel music by which a troubled breast can be soothed. Jesus Christ's teaching is still the best news of these days, as it was centuries ago. Though the world has had nearly 1900 years of the glad tidings, the gospel hath the dew of its youth upon it, and when men hear it they still ask, as the Greeks did of old,

'What new doctrine is this?' Our Lord Jesus has come to set up, by the preaching and teaching of the gospel, a new kingdom, a kingdom having new laws, new customs, a new charter, and new riches, a kingdom which is not of this world, a kingdom founded upon better principles and bringing infinitely better results to its subjects than any other dominion that hath ever been. Into that kingdom he introduces only new men, who are made new creatures in Christ Jesus, who therefore love his new commandment and serve him in newness of spirit and not in the oldness of the letter. Moreover, Christ hath opened for us an entrance into the kingdom of heaven above, for now we come to God 'by a new and living way, which he hath consecrated for us through the veil, that is to say, his flesh.' When in days to come we shall meet him again there will still be novelty, for he has said, 'I will not drink henceforth of the fruit of the vine until that day when I drink it new with you in my Father's kingdom.' Indeed, concerning our Lord and Master everything is new, and was it not so prophesied? For did not Isaiah say, in the forty-third chapter, eighteenth verse, 'Remember ye not the former things, neither consider the things of old. Behold, I will do a new thing; now it shall spring forth; shall ye not know it?.' And to the same effect was his prophecy in the sixty-fifth chapter, seventeenth verse: 'For, behold, I create new heavens and a new earth: and the former shall not be remembered, nor come into mind. But be ye glad and rejoice for ever in that which I create: for, behold, I create Jerusalem a rejoicing, and her people a joy.' This newness of everything was to be a leading feature in Messiah's reign, and it has already been so; but far more shall this be seen in the latter days. Doth not John in Revelation 21: 5 say, 'He that sat upon the throne said, Behold, I make all things new.' Foretold in former ages as the Creator of new heavens and new earth, our Lord shall at last, in the summing up, be plainly seen to be the Maker of all things new. Do you wonder, beloved, that if a man be in Christ he is a new creature? If everything that Christ touches is made new, if he refreshes and revives, if he re-establishes and re-edifies, and new-creates wherever he goes, are you at all astonished that those who live nearest to his heart, nay, are in vital union with his blessed person, should also be made new? It would be very astonishing if it were not so.

Let us direct our attention then to the teaching of the text, 'If any man be in Christ, he is a new creature.'

1. We shall first consider with brevity THE GROUND OF THE NOVELTY which is here spoken of. It is, 'If any man be *in Christ* he is a new creature,' not otherwise. No man cometh to be a new creature by any process apart from Christ. 'If any man be in Christ, he is a new creature,' but if any man be not in Christ he is not a new creature, nor can he become so except by connection with him of whom it is written that he is 'the beginning of the creation of God.' As in the old creation 'without him was not anything made that was made,' so is it in the new. He maketh all things new, but the things that are apart from him have waxen old and are ready to perish, neither can they renew their youth. As well might the face of the earth hope to be renewed with spring apart from the sun, as for a soul to hope for spiritual renewal apart from Jesus. The wonderful newness produced by re-generation and new creation is the work of the Holy Ghost and his operations are all in union with the Lord Jesus and aimed at his glory. 'He that believeth on the Son hath everlasting life: and he that believeth not the Son shall not see life, but the wrath of God

abideth on him.'

But how cometh it that a man is indeed a new creature if he be in Christ? I answer, first, it cometh necessarily from *the representative character of Christ* towards those who are in him. If you wanted a man to be made a new creature, and were omnipotent, what process would suggest itself to you? I think a double one. To make an old creature into a new creature there must first be the stroke which ends him, and then the touch which begins him anew: to put it more plainly, there must be death and then life. Now, has that taken place upon those who are in Christ? Of course it has, if it has taken place upon Christ himself, because he is the Head, and represents the members. As Adam acted for the seed in him, so Christ hath acted for the seed in him. See, then, beloved, Christ hath died; he came before the judgement seat with our sins upon him, the representative of those of whom he is the head; and in him death, which was the penalty of sin, was fulfilled to the letter, its bitterest dregs being drunk up. Jesus died. We are certain that he died, for the executioners brake not his legs because they saw that he was dead already, but one of the soldiers with a spear pierced his side, and forthwith came there out blood and water. We know that he died, for the jealous eyes of his enemies would not have permitted him to have been taken down from the cross unless the life had assuredly departed. He was laid in the grave, assuredly dead, under the dominion of death for the time being; and you and I who are in him, at that time died in him. 'If one died for all then all died.' Such is the proper translation of that passage. We died, for he died in our name. Our sin was punished in him by the death which he endured. See ye, then, brethren, we are dead, dead by virtue of our federal union with Jesus Christ. I mean not you all, unless ye are all in Christ

Jesus. Judge ye whether it be so with you or not. But I mean as many as the Father gave to Christ, as many as Christ in his intent did specially redeem by becoming their substitute: these were in him, and in him they died, being crucified with him. In him also all his people rose again when he rose. On the third day he burst the bonds of death and left the grave on our behalf. See how the Holy Spirit, by his servant Paul, identifies us with all this. 'Now if we be dead with Christ, we believe that we shall also live with him: knowing that Christ being raised from the dead dieth no more; death hath no more dominion over him. For in that he died, he died unto sin once: but in that he liveth, he liveth unto God. Likewise reckon ye also yourselves to be dead indeed unto sin, but alive unto God through Jesus Christ our Lord.' As far as he was our representative he was a new man when he rose. The law had no claims upon him: he had been dead, and so had passed out of its jurisdiction. The law never had any claim upon the risen Christ: it had a claim upon him when he came under the law, but when he had satisfied it to the last jot and tittle, by death, he was completely clear. Hath the law of our country any claim upon a man after he is dead? If a dead man can be raised again all his past offences are done with, he beginneth a new life, and is not under the old law. And so with Christ and so with us, for here is the point of union, we are risen with him by faith of the resurrection of Christ. We have been dead and buried, and now we are risen, and thus this, which is the very best and surest process for making a person a new creature, has been undergone by all God's elect, by reason of the representative and sacrificial death of Jesus Christ and his glorious representative resurrection on their behalf.

But, beloved, there is another meaning. *We are*

made new creatures by an actual process as well as by the legal process which I have described, and here also the same thing is done. We are made vitally one with Jesus Christ when we believe in him, and then do we spiritually die and are made to live again. Our faith apprehends the dying of Christ and we feel at the same time the sentence of death in ourselves. We see how we deserve to die for sin, and we accept the sentence, confessing our guiltiness before the Most High, and there is proclaimed throughout the powers and passions of the soul the decree from God that the flesh shall die, with all its lusts. We write down sin as henceforth dead to us, and ourselves as dead to it. We labour to mortify all our evil desires and the lusts of the flesh and all that cometh of the flesh. When we believe in Jesus a sword goes through the very loins of sin, and the arrows of the Lord stick fast in the hearts of the King's enemies that lurk within our spirit. There also cometh a new life into us as we behold Jesus risen from the dead. When we believe in Jesus we receive from God a new vital principle, of superior and heavenly character, akin to Deity; there droppeth into our soul a sacred seed from the hand of the eternal Spirit, living and incorruptible, which abideth for ever, and for ever bringeth forth fruit after its kind. As we believe in Christ living we live in Christ and live after the fashion of Christ, and the Spirit of him that raised up Christ from the dead dwelleth in our mortal bodies, making us to live in newness of life.

Now, beloved, do you know anything about this? Have you been made new creatures by death and resurrection? If you have been baptized you have professed that so it has been with you. 'Know ye not, that so many of us as were baptized into Jesus Christ were baptized into his death? Therefore we are buried with him by baptism into death: that like as Christ was raised up from the dead by the glory of the Father, even so we also should walk in newness of life. For if we have been planted together in the likeness of his death, we shall be also in the likeness of his resurrection.' In the ordinance of baptism, by burial in the water, and uprising from it, there is a setting forth as in a type and figure of our Lord's burial and resurrection, and at the same time it is an emblem of the process by which we become new creatures in him. But is it *really* so in your souls? Are you now henceforth dead to the world, and dead to sin, and quickened into the life of Christ? If you be so, then the text will bear to you a third and practical meaning, for it will not merely be true that your old man is condemned to die and a new nature is bestowed, but *in your common actions you will try to show this by newness of actual conversation.* Evils which tempted you at one time will be unable to beguile you now because you are dead to them: the charms of the painted face of the world will no longer attract your attention, for your eyes are blind to such deceitful beauties. You have obtained a new life which can only be satisfied by new delights, which can be excited by new objects and constrained by new principles suitable to its own nature. This you will continually show. The life of God within you will make your actions instinct with holiness, and the end thereof shall be everlasting life. Your faith in Christ clearly evinces you to be a new creature, for it kills your old confidences and makes you build upon a new basis: your love to Christ also shows your newness, for it has slain your old affections and captured your heart for Jesus only: and your hope, which is also a gift of the blessed Spirit, is set upon new things altogether, while your old hopes are things whereof you are now ashamed.

Thus it is that first by the headship of Christ you are legally dead and alive again; next by your vital union with Christ you are dead and alive again as a matter of experience, and now it is practically proven in your life from day to day that you are dead and your life is hid with Christ in God: in all these three ways you are new creatures by the double process of dying and quickening. You are under a new Adam, and so start life afresh as new creatures; you are under a new covenant, and commence to act under different principles, and so are new creatures: you are quickened by a new Spirit, and so in thought and word and deed are seen to be new creatures. But all this is *in Christ,* and if you are not in Christ you are still in the old world which must shortly be destroyed. As 'by the Word of God were the heavens made, and all the host of them by the breath of his mouth,' so have you been created by Jesus, the Eternal Word, and quickened by his Spirit, or else you still abide in death. If your faith has never laid her hand upon Christ's sacrifice for sin then your soul has never felt the regenerating influence of the Holy Spirit, and all the baptismal regeneration and all else of human invention that may now comfort you is but a vain deceit. Ye must be born again, but it can only be in Christ Jesus, for to 'as many as received him, to them gave he power to become the sons of God, even to them that believe on his name.' 'He that hath the Son hath life; and he that hath not the Son of God hath not life.' O that we may all believe in him, and enter into the new life.

'Author of the new creation,
    Come with all thy Spirit's power;
Make our hearts thy habitation,
    On our souls thy graces shower.'

2. I shall in the second place lead you to consider the ESSENCE OF THIS NOVELTY. 'If any man be in Christ, he is *a new creature.*' Read, and the reading will be accurate, 'He is a new creation.' This is a very sweeping statement. A man in Christ is not the old man purified, nor the old man improved, nor the old man in a better humour, nor the old man with additions and subtractions, nor the old man dressed in gorgeous robes. No, he is a new creature altogether. As for the old man, what is to be done with him? Can he not be sobered, reformed, and made to do us useful service? No, he is crucified with Christ, and bound to die by a lingering but certain death. The capital sentence is passed upon him, for he cannot be mended and therefore must be ended. 'The carnal mind is enmity against God: for it is not subject to the law of God, neither indeed can be.' You cannot change the old nature, it is immutably bad, and the sooner it is put away as a filthy and unclean thing the better for us. The believer, so far as he is in Christ, is a new creation: not the old stuff put into a new fashion, and the old material worked up into an improved form, but absolutely a new creation. To create is to make out of nothing, and that is precisely how the newborn life came into us; it is not a development, or an outgrowth, but a creation, a heavenly something called into being by a power from above. The new man in us is made out of nothing that was in us before, for nature does not assist grace, but is opposed to it. Christ has not found light stored away in our darkness, nor life amid the corruption of our spiritual death. The new birth is from above, and the life produced thereby is a new creation, and not the goodness of nature educated till it becomes grace. They are getting up a notion in certain quarters that the children of pious parents, if not of all mankind, are the

children of God by their first birth, and only want certain training and influences to be brought to bear upon them and then they will develop into Christians as they grow up into manhood and womanhood. One divine says that our children ought not to need conversion. This theory is false throughout, for the best of children are by nature heirs of wrath even as others. The grace of God in the soul is a new creation, and not the natural development of a pious education and training working upon the innate goodness of men: indeed there is no such goodness there at all; it is a vainglorious dream and nothing more. The new man in Christ is not the old creature washed and put out to school, and elevated by 'modern thought and culture.' No; the Ethiopian cannot change his skin, nor the leopard his spots; do what you will with him he will be an Ethiopian and a leopard still; but the new man in Christ is another creature altogether.

Mark you, it is not said that the man has something new about him, but he, himself, is new. It is not merely that in a spiritual sense he has new eyes, new hands and new feet, but he himself, is a new creation. Mark that. Do you not see then that salvation is the work of God? You cannot create yourself, and you cannot create anything at all. Try and create a fly first, and then you may dream of being able to create a new heart and a right spirit in another person, but even then it would be quite another matter to new create yourself. Is not the very idea an absurdity? Shall nothing create something? Shall darkness create light? Shall sin create holiness? Shall death create life? Shall the devil create God? None of these questions are more absurd than the idea of the sinner's being able to new create himself.

No, beloved, regeneration is an extraordinary work, demanding omnipotence to accomplish it; it is, in fact, a divine work, for it is the supreme prerogative of God to create.

> 'Know that the Lord is God alone,
> He can create, and he destroy.'

If any man be in Christ it is not only said that he is a creation, but a *new creation,* and the word here translated 'new,' as has been well observed, does not signify *recent,* but something altogether different from that which previously existed. A book may be new, and yet it may be only a fresh copy of some old work; but that is not the case in this instance. The creature is not a new specimen of the same kind as the old, but another and different creation. We might almost read the text as if it said, 'If any man be in Christ he is a fresh creation, a new kind of creature altogether.' The new creation differs essentially from the old, although the first is an instructive emblem of the second. The first creation was the work of physical power, the second a work of spiritual power: the first created for the most part materialism in its various forms, but the new creation deals with spiritual things, and manifests the sublimest attributes of the divine character. God in nature is glorious, but in grace he is all glorious. The second is a creation nearer to the heart of God than the first creation was; for when he made the world he simply said it was good, but when he makes the new creation, it is written, 'He shall rest in his love; he shall rejoice over thee with singing.' So gladdening to his heart is the sight of the new creature which his grace hath made, that he sings a joyful hymn.

Furthermore, we must note that if any man be in Christ he is a new creature, and the creation of him bears some resemblance to the creation of the world. I have at other times gone through that wonderful first chapter of the Book of Genesis, which is a Bible in miniature, and I have tried to show how it sets forth the spiritual creation. Behold by nature we lie like chaos: a mass of disorder, confusion and darkness. As in the old creation so in the new, the Spirit of God broodeth over us and moveth upon the face of all things. Then the word of the Lord comes and says within us, as aforetime in chaos and old night, 'Let there be light,' and there is light. After light there comes a division of the light from the darkness, and we learn to call them by their names. The light is 'day' and the darkness is 'night.' So to us there is a knowing and a naming of things, and a discerning of differences in matters which before we confounded when we put light for darkness. After a while there cometh forth in us the lower forms of spiritual life. As in the earth there came grasses and herbs, so in us there come desire, hope and sorrow for sin. By and by there appeared on the globe fowl and fish, and beasts, and living things, and life beyond all count. So also in the new creation, from having life we go on to have it more abundantly. God by degrees created all his works, till at last he had finished all the host of them, and even so he works on till he completes in us the new creation and looks upon us with rejoicing. Then he bringeth to us a day of rest, blessing us and causing us to enter into his rest because of his finished work. We could draw a very beautiful parallel if we had time, but you can think it out for yourselves.

Now, notice very carefully that if *any* man be in Christ he is a new creature, and this certifies that a new creation has taken place upon every man who is in Christ, whether by nature he was a Jew or Gentile, a moralist or a rake, a philosopher or a fool. When a man is converted and brought to Christ he has invariably become a new creature. If he has believed in

Jesus only three minutes yet he is a new creature; and if he hath known the Lord seventy years he can be no more. A new creation is a new creature, and in this matter there is no difference between the babe in grace and the father in Israel. As this creation is common to all the saints, so is it *immediate and present.* 'If any man be in Christ he is a new creature': it is not spoken of as a something that is to happen to him in the last article of death, wherein some seem to hope that many wonderful changes will be wrought in them; but he who is in Christ is a new creature *now.* 'Neither circumcision nor uncircumcision availeth anything, but a new creature': and that new creature is now possessed, and I may add consciously possessed too: for albeit that there may arise occasional doubts upon this question, yet in a man's inmost self he finds cause to know that there has passed upon him a marvellous change which only God himself could have wrought.

This change is *universal in the man;* the new man is not full grown in every part, nor in fact in any part, and yet in all the portions of his regenerated nature he is a new creature. I mean this, if any man be in Christ it is not his mental *eye* that is a new creation merely, but he himself is a new creation. He has a new heart according to the promise, 'A new heart also will I give you, and a new spirit will I put within you.' He hath new ears, hearing what he refused to hear before; he has a new tongue, and can pray with it as he never prayed before; he has new feet, and these delight to run in the ways of God's commandments. I refer of course only to his inner man, that is altogether new, and not any one part of it only. If a man be merely enlightened in understanding, what is that? It is good, but it is not salvation; a new brain is not all that is wanted to make a new man. A new man is spiritually new created from head to foot. Though but a babe in grace, and not fully developed in any one part, yet he is new 'created in Christ Jesus unto good works which God hath before ordained that we should walk in them.'

Thus have I tried to show you the essence of the novelty.

3. Let us next consider THE EXTENT OF THE NOVELTY. 'If any man be in Christ he is a new creature; *old things are passed away, behold all things have become new.'* It seems then that not only is the man a new creature, but he has entered into a new creation; he has opened his eyes in a new world. Imagine Adam falling asleep at the gates of Paradise just under the cherubim's flaming sword, with the thorns and thistles springing up before him: and then the serpent's trail behind him: and then further picture him lying there in a deep sleep till the Lord touches him, makes him open his eyes, and causes him to find himself in a better paradise than the one he had lost. It was not so in reality, but can you imagine such a thing? If so, it may serve as a symbol of what the Lord has done for us. We are made new, and find ourselves in a new world. What about *the old things?* The text says they have passed away, and the Greek word gives the idea of their having passed away spontaneously. I cannot liken it to anything that I know of better than the snow which melts in the sun. You wake up one morning, and all the trees are festooned with snowy wreaths, while down below upon the ground the snow lies in a white sheet over everything. Lo, the sun has risen, its beams shed a genial warmth; and in a few hours where is the snow? It has passed away. Had you hired a thousand carts and horses and machines to sweep it away it could not have been more effectually removed. It has passed away. That is what the Lord does in the new creation: his love shines on the soul,

his grace renews us, and the old things pass away as a matter of course. Where are your old views about which you used to be so positive? Where are those old opinions for which you could freely have knocked a man down? Where are those old sneers against God's people? Where are those old pleasures which you took so much delight in? Where are those old engrossing pursuits? Had you a hard tug to get away from these bonds? Where are those old joys, those old hopes, those old trusts, those old confidences? Was it difficult to shake off these? Ah, no! Beneath the power of the Holy Spirit they have passed away. You hardly know how it is, but they have gone, and gone completely. As a dream when one awaketh you have despised their image, and your heart knows them no more. It is marvellous in this new creation how the Lord makes confusion and the old night to fly. You may call for them and say, 'Chaos, where art thou?' and no answer comes back, for old things are passed away. Our Lord Jesus Christ causes all this. Where his blessed face beams with grace and truth, as the sun with warmth and light, he dissolves the bands of sin's long frost, and brings on the spring of grace with newness of buds and flowers.

But when you remove the old what is to take its place? Do you not observe that *new things have come*: 'Behold all things are become new.' Now the man has new views, new notions, new ambitions, new convictions, new desires, new hopes, new dreads, new aims, new principles, and new affections: he is led by a new spirit and follows a new course of life; everything in fact about him is as if he had come fresh from the hand of God. Even as with the cleansed leper, his flesh came again to him as the flesh of a little child, and he was clean, so is it with the heart renewed by grace.

Beloved, it is delightful to read in the Book of

Revelation and anticipate the things which are to be hereafter. How full that book is of novelties which illustrate our subject, for there you read of a new name which the Lord bestows upon those who overcome. Perhaps some of you used actually to be known by some nickname or vulgar epithet while you lived in the world and were a lover of it. Now in all probability you are called by quite a different name among your Christian friends. Saul the persecutor is called Paul when he becomes an apostle. Moreover, there is a new name, which the mouth of the Lord shall name, which no man knoweth saving he that receiveth it. You have been named with the name of the Father, and of the Son, and of the Holy Ghost, and you wear henceforth that name by which the whole family in heaven and earth is named. Grace also has taught you a *new song*: 'He hath put a new song into my mouth and established my goings.' You are rehearsing the music of that glorious band of whom it is written, 'They sang a new song, saying, Thou art worthy to take the book and to open the seals thereof.' Now are you a citizen of a *new city,* the new Jerusalem which cometh down out of heaven from God, which shall be established among the sons of men, in the last days as the world's metropolis, concerning which they shall say, 'The temple of God is with men and he doth dwell among them.'

Beloved, each one of you has now become part of *one new man.* Do you know what I mean by that? There were once the Jews and the Gentiles, but now, saith Paul, Christ 'hath broken down the middle wall of partition; for to make in himself of twain one new man, so making peace.' The mystical body of Christ is the one new man, and we are members of that body. Henceforth we have communion with all saints, and to us 'there is neither Greek nor Jew, bond nor free, but

Christ is all and in all.' Even now we have commenced to live in a new heaven and walk upon a new earth, and we are anticipating the time when literally on this very earth whereon we have struggled there shall be set up a new condition of things, for the first heaven and the first earth shall have passed away and there shall be no more sea. Rolled up like a scroll shall yon blue heavens be, and the elements shall melt with fervent heat; nevertheless, we, according to his promise, look for new heavens and a new earth, to which in expectation we are always drawing near, and pressing forward with inward yearning, for already in Christ Jesus we are a part of that new creation which is more fully to be revealed.

4. Fourthly let us consider THE RESULT OF THIS NOVELTY. 'If any man be in Christ, he is a new creature.' Well, the result of this novelty is, first, that the man is already a great wonder to himself. You know the Pythagorean doctrine of the transmigration of souls, the soul passing first into one body and then into another, and so existing under different conditions. We do not believe that fiction for a moment, but if it had been true, the memories of such souls must have been stored with varied information, surpassingly strange to hear. Ours is another transformation, it is death and resurrection: the old passing away and the new being created: but how remarkable are the experiences of the men who have been so transformed! Here is a man who is a new creature, and he has a very distinct recollection of the time when he was something far other than he now is. What a change he has undergone! Supposing a swine could suddenly be turned into a man and yet recollect what it did when it was one of the herd; what an experience it would have to tell! If you could take a hog from the trough and turn it into an emperor, that would not be

half so great a change as is accomplished when an unregenerated sinner becomes a saint; but I warrant you the emperor would not find much cause for glorifying in his former swinish state; he would be silent and ashamed when others mentioned it. If he alluded to that state it would always be with the blushes of humiliation and the tears of gratitude. If anybody began to talk about it, and he knew that there might be others about him that might be helped by hearing what the Lord had done, he would begin to tell in a gentle, modest way how the Lord tranformed him from a swine into a monarch, but he would never, never boast: how could he? In such a case the poor swine would have no responsibility and could not be blamed for wallowing in the mire, but this cannot be said of us; for when we acted as swine we knew better, and sinned wilfully. Still, what a change it is! How I wonder at myself! How I marvel at the goodness of my God! How I adore that sacred power which has made me the child of two births, the subject of two creations: he first made me in the fashion of a man, and then made me in the image of the man Christ Jesus. I was first born to die, and then born to live eternally. Let us bless God and be full of lowly wonder this morning.

The next result of this new creation is, however, that the man does not feel at home in this present evil world, for this is the old creation, and the new man, the twice-born man, feels as if he were out of his element and not in a congenial country. He dwells in a body which is nothing better than a frail, uncomfortable, easily removed tent, in which he groans, earnestly desiring to enter his own house at home, the house not made with hands, eternal in the heavens. Wherever he goes things seem out of order with the rule which is set up in his soul. He loves not the world, neither the things in the world; the world's glories do not charm him, and its treasures do not enchant him. Earth's music grates upon his refined ear, which is tuned to heavenly harmony; its dainties do not delight the taste, which has learned to enjoy the bread of heaven. The new creatures pine to be in the new creation. And beloved, while we are pining we are preparing: the Spirit of God is working us to this selfsame thing, and filling us with groans and pangs of strong desire, which indicate that we are becoming more and more fit to be partakers with the saints in light, who see the face of the Beloved without a veil, and drink in ever new delights.

Mark you once more, while the new creature is thus watching and waiting for the new creation he is meanwhile extending an influence more or less unconscious over the old world in which he dwells. Just as our Lord has gone to heaven to prepare a place for us, so we, his people, are stopping here to prepare a place for him. We are winning men from the world to Christ, we are raising the tone of morals, we are spreading light and truth on all sides by the power of the Spirit, and so we are helping to make the world readier to receive the great King. We are seeking out his jewels, we are bringing his rebellious subjects to his feet. The life that is in us seems out of place in this mortal frame, for the body is dead because of sin, and therefore we groan, being burdened. As for the world itself, it is not our rest, for it is polluted. It seems a dreadful thing for the living Spirit to be dwelling in this graveyard of a world, but there is a necessity for us to be here. We are linked with a creation made subject to vanity, because it was thus subjected, not willingly, but by reason of him who hath subjected the same in hope that the creation itself also 'shall be delivered from the bondage of corruption into the glorious liberty of the children of God.' We are here as links between the spiritual and the material, and we are working out divine purposes for the fuller display of the divine glory. Wherefore comfort one another with these words, and as new creatures in Jesus Christ look for the new heavens and the new earth, and for the coming of your Lord and Saviour. Know ye not that when he shall appear then shall ye also appear with him in glory. Let us even now bow before him and salute him with the language of our hymn.

> 'To thee the world its treasure brings;
>   To thee its mighty bow;
> To thee the church exulting springs;
>   Her Sovereign, Saviour Thou!

> 'Beneath thy touch, beneath thy smile,
>   New heavens and earth appear;
> No sin their beauty to defile,
>   Nor dim them with a tear.'

CHRIST
THE SPOILER OF
PRINCIPALITIES AND
POWERS

*'And having spoiled principalities and powers, he made
a shew of them openly, triumphing over them in it.'*
– Colossians 2:15

To the eye of reason the cross is the centre of sorrow
and the lowest depth of shame. Jesus dies a mal-
efactor's death. In the midst of mockery, and jest, and
scorn, and blasphemy, he gives up the ghost. Earth
rejects him and lifts him from her surface, and heaven
affords him no light, but darkens the mid-day sun in
the hour of his extremity. To the world the cross must
ever be the emblem of shame; to the Jew a stumbling-
block, and to the Greek foolishness. How different,
however, is the view which presents itself to the eye of
faith. Faith knows no shame in the cross, except the
shame of the sin which nailed the Saviour there; it sees
no ground for scorn, but pours contempt on all de-
spisers. Faith sees, indeed, a dying Saviour, but it
beholds him bringing life and immortality to light at
the moment when his soul is eclipsed in the shadow of
death. Faith regards the cross, not as the emblem of
shame, but as the token of glory. The sons of Belial lay
the cross in the dust, but the Christian makes a con-
stellation of it, and sees it glittering in the seventh
heaven.

My brethren, our text tells us that the cross was
our Lord's field of triumph: there he fought, and
conquered, too. As a victor, on the cross he divided
the spoil. Nay, more than this; in our text the cross is

spoken of as being Christ's triumphal chariot in which he rode when he led captivity captive, and received gifts for men. Calvin thus admirably expounds the last sentence of our text: 'The expression in the Greek allows, it is true, of the reading *in himself;* the connection of the passage, however, requires that we read it otherwise; for what would be meagre as applied to Christ, suits admirably well as applied to the cross. For as he had previously compared the cross to a signal trophy or show of triumph, in which Christ led about his enemies, so he now also compares it to a triumphal car in which he showed himself in great magnificence. For there is no tribunal so magnificent, no throne so stately, no show of triumph so distinguished, no chariot so elevated, as is the gibbet on which Christ has subdued death and the devil, the prince of death; nay, more, has utterly trodden them under his feet.'

First, I shall at this time endeavour to describe *Christ as spoiling his enemies on the cross;* and having done that, I shall lead you to see *the Saviour leading his foes captive in triumphal procession upon and through his cross,* there and then making a show of them openly, triumphing over them in it.

1. First, our faith is invited to behold CHRIST ON THE CROSS MAKING A SPOIL OF PRINCIPALITIES AND POWERS. Satan, leagued with sin and death, had made this world a dungeon of woe. The prince of the power of the air, fell usurper, not content with his dominions in hell, must needs invade this fair earth. He found our first parents in the bliss of Eden; he tempted them to forego their allegiance to the King of heaven; and they became his bondslaves – bondslaves for ever, if the Lord of heaven had not interposed to ransom them. The voice of mercy was heard while the fetters were being riveted upon their

feet, crying, 'Ye shall yet be free. He who shall bruise the serpent's head shall deliver his prisoners from the house of bondage.'

Long did the promise tarry. At last, in the fulness of time, the Deliverer appeared, and after a life of conflict, came to closer quarters with the foe. He entered on the battle saying, 'This is your hour and the power of darkness. Now is the crisis of this world; now must the prince of darkness be cast out.' From the table of communion the Redeemer arose at midnight, and marched forth to the battle. How dreadful was the contest! In the first onset the champion appeared to be vanquished. Beaten to the earth at the first assault, he fell upon his knees and cried, 'My Father, if it be possible let this cup pass from me.' Revived in strength, made strong by heaven, he no longer feared or uttered a word which looked like renouncing the fight. From the terrible skirmish, all red with bloody sweat, he dashed into the thick of the fight. The kiss of Judas was, as it were, the first sounding of the trumpet; Pilate's bar was the unsheathing of the weapons; the cruel lash was the crossing of the swords: but the cross was the centre of the battle; there, on the top of Calvary, must the dread fight of eternity be fought. Now must the Son of God arise, and gird his sword upon his thigh.

Dread defeat or glorious conquest awaited the champion of the church. Which shall it be? We hold our breath with anxious suspense while the storm is raging. The howls and yells of hell rise in awful clamour. The pit is emptying out its legions. Terrible as lions, hungry as wolves and black as night, the demons rush on in myriads. Satan's reserved forces, those that had long been kept against this day of terrible battle, are roaring from their dens. Countless are their armies, and fierce their countenances. Brandishing his sword the arch fiend leads the van, bidding his followers fight neither with small nor great, save only with the King of Israel. Terrible are the leaders of the battle. Sin is there, and all its innumerable off-spring, spitting forth the venom of asps, and infixing their poisoned fangs in the Saviour's flesh. Death is there upon his pale horse, and his cruel dart rends its way through the body of Jesus even to his inmost heart. The Lord is 'exceeding sorrowful, even unto death.' Hell is there with coals of juniper and fiery darts. But chief and head amongst them is Satan; remembering well the ancient day when Christ hurled him from the battlements of heaven, he rushes with all his malice yelling to the attack. The darts shot into the air, are so countless that they blind the sun. Darkness covers the battlefield, even darkness which might be felt. Long does the conflict seem to waver, the fight of one against many. One man – nay, tell it, lest any should misunderstand me, *the one God* stands in battle array against ten thousands of principalities and powers. On, on they come, and he bears the shock of all. Silently at first he permits their ranks to break upon him, too terribly enduring hardness to spare a thought for shouting. But at last the battlecry is heard. He who is fighting for his people lifts up his voice, but it is a cry which makes his friends to tremble. The battle is so hot upon him and the dust so thick that he is choked with thirst. He cries, 'I thirst.' Surely, now he is about to be defeated! Wait a while! See ye yon heaps; all these have fallen beneath his arm! as for the rest, fear not the issue. The enemy is but rushing to his own destruction. In vain his fury and his rage; for see, the last rank is charging: the battle of ages is almost over. At last the darkness is dispersed and with it the legions of his foes. Hark how the conqueror cries, 'It is finished.' And where are now his enemies? They are all dead. There lies the king of terrors, pierced through with one of his own darts! There lies Satan with his head broken! Yonder crawls the broken-backed serpent, writhing in ghastly misery! As for sin, it is cut in pieces and scattered to the winds of heaven! '*It is finished*,' cries the conqueror, as he returns with dyed garments from Bozrah: 'I have trodden the winepress alone, I have trampled them in my fury, and their blood has stained all my raiment.'

Behold he proceeds to *divide the spoil*, and we are glad to remember that when the spoil is divided it is a sure token that the warfare is accomplished. The enemy will never suffer the spoil to be divided among the conquerors as long as he has any strength remaining. We may gather from our text of a surety, that Jesus Christ has totally routed all his enemies.

What means this metaphor of Christ dividing the spoil? I take it that it means, first of all, that *he disarmed all his enemies*. Satan came against Christ; he had in his hand a sharp sword called the Law, dipped in the poison of sin, so that every wound which the law inflicted was deadly. Christ dashed this sword out of Satan's hand, and there stood the prince of darkness unarmed. His helmet was cleft in twain, and his head was crushed as with a rod of iron. Death also rose against Christ, but the Saviour snatched his quiver from him, emptied out all his darts, cut them in two, and gave him back the feather end, but kept the poisoned barbs from him, that he might never destroy the ransomed. Sin came against Christ! But sin was utterly cut in pieces. It had been Satan's armour-bearer, but its shield was cast away, and it lay dead upon the plain. Satan has nothing left him now wherewith he may mortally wound us, for his sword is broken to shivers. In battles of old, especially among the Romans, after the enemy had been overcome, it was the custom to take away all their weapons and ammunition; afterwards they were stripped of their armour and their garments, their hands were tied behind their backs, and they were made to pass under the yoke. Even so hath Christ done with sin, death and hell; he hath taken their armour, spoiled them of their weapons, and made them pass under the yoke; captivity is led captive.

In the next place, *he took away their treasures*, as well as their weapons. Victors impoverish, and so weaken, their defeated foes. They dismantle their fortresses, and rifle all their stores, so that they may not be able to renew the attack. Christ hath done the like with all his enemies. Satan had taken away from us all our possessions: all the joy, and happiness, and peace of man, Satan had taken. Not that he could enjoy them himself, but that he delighted to ruin us. Christ has gotten back to us our lost inheritance. Paradise is ours, and more. O robber of our race, how art thou spoiled! Didst thou deprive Adam of his riches? The second Adam hath rent them from thee! How is the hammer of the whole earth cut asunder and broken, and the waster is become desolate. Now shall the needy be remembered, and again shall the meek inherit the earth. 'Then is the prey of a great spoil divided; the lame take the prey.'

Moreover, when victors divide the spoil, it is usual to *take away all the ornaments* from the enemy, their crowns and their jewels. Christ on the cross did the like with Satan. Satan wore a haughty diadem of triumph. 'I fought the first Adam,' he said, 'I overcame him, and here's my glittering coronet.' Christ snatched it from his brow in the hour when he bruised his head. And now Satan cannot boast of a single victory, he is thoroughly defeated. In the first skirmish he defeated manhood, but in the second battle manhood vanquished him. Satan's reigning power is gone. He may tempt, but he cannot compel; he may threaten, but he cannot subdue; for the crown is taken from his head, and the mighty are brought low. O sing unto the Lord a new song, all ye his people, make a joyful noise unto him with psalms, all ye his redeemed; for he hath dashed in pieces the enemy.

And now, what says this to us? Simply this. If Christ on the cross hath spoiled Satan, let us not be afraid to encounter this great enemy of our souls. My brethren, in all things we must be made like unto Christ. We must bear our cross, and on that cross we must fight as he did with sin, and death and hell. Let us not fear. The result of the battle is certain, for as the Lord our Saviour hath overcome once for all, even so shall we most surely conquer in him. Be ye not afraid with sudden fear when the evil one cometh upon you. If he accuse you, reply to him in these words – 'Who shall lay anything to the charge of God's elect?' If he condemn you, laugh him to scorn, crying – 'Who is he that condemneth? It is Christ that died, yea rather, that is risen again.' If he threaten to divide you from Christ's love, encounter him with confidence, for 'I am persuaded, that neither things present, nor things to come, nor height, nor depth, nor any other creature, shall be able to separate us from the love of God which is in Christ Jesus our Lord.' If he let loose your sins upon you, dash the hell-dogs aside with this – 'If any man sin, *we* have an advocate with the Father, Jesus Christ the righteous.' If death should threaten you, shout in his very face – 'O death, where is thy sting? O grave, where is thy victory?' Hold up the cross before you. Let that be your shield and buckler, and rest assured that as your Master not only routed the foe but afterwards took the spoil, it shall be even so with you. Your battles with Satan shall turn to your advantage. You shall become all the richer for your antagonists. The more numerous your afflictions the greater your share of the spoil. Your tribulation shall work patience, and your patience experience, and your experience hope – a hope that maketh not ashamed. By the very attacks of Satan shall you be helped the better to enjoy the rest which remaineth to the people of God. Put yourselves in array against sin and Satan. All ye that bend the bow, shoot at them: spare no arrows, for your enemies are rebels against God. Fear not, neither be ye dismayed, for the battle is the Lord's and he will deliver them into your hands.

2. The second part of our text refers to OUR LORD'S TRIUMPH ON THE CROSS. When a Roman general had performed great feats in a foreign country, his highest reward was that the senate should decree him a triumph. On a certain set day the gates of Rome were thrown open; the houses were all decorated, and the people climbed to the tops of the houses, or stood in great crowds along the streets. The gates were opened, and by-and-by the first legion began to stream in with its banners flying, and its trumpets sounding. The people saw the stern warriors as they marched along the street returning from the blood-red battlefields. After one half of the army had thus defiled, your eye would rest upon one who was the centre of all attraction. Riding in a noble chariot drawn by milk-white horses, there came the conqueror himself, crowned with the laurel crown and standing erect. Chained to his chariot were the kings and mighty men of the regions which he had conquered. Immediately behind them came part of the booty. There were carried the ivory and the ebony, the gold and silver vessels, and rare fabrics, together with the beasts of the different countries which he had sub-dued. After these came the rest of the soldiery, a long,

long stream of valiant men, all of them sharing the triumph of their captain. Behind them came banners, the old flags which had floated aloft in battle, and the standards which had been taken from the enemy. After these, men bore aloft painted emblems of the great victories of the warrior. Upon one there would be a huge map depicting the rivers which he had crossed, or the seas through which his navy had found their way. Everything was represented in a picture, and the populace gave a fresh shout as they saw the memorial of each victory. Behind, together with other trophies, would come the prisoners of less eminent rank. Then the rear would be closed with trumpeters sounding aloud and swelling the acclamations of the throng. It was a noble day for old Rome. Children would never forget those glorious shows and galas; they would estimate their years from the time of one triumph to another. High holiday was kept in the great warrior's name. Women cast down flowers before the hero, and he was the monarch of the day.

Now, our apostle had evidently seen such a triumph, or read of it, and he takes this as a representation of what Christ did on the cross. 'He made a show of them openly, triumphing over them in it.' How could the cross be the scene of a triumph? Most of the old commentators can scarcely conceive it to be true. They say, 'This must certainly refer to Christ's resurrection and ascension.' But, nevertheless, so saith the Scripture, even on the cross Christ triumphed over his foes. Yes! While those hands were bleeding, the acclamations of angels were being poured upon his head. Yes, while those feet were being rent with the nails, the noblest spirits in the world were crowding round him with admiration. And when upon that blood-stained cross he died in agonies unutterable, there went up a shout of acclamation such as never was heard before, for the ransomed in heaven, and all the angels of God with loudest harmony chanted his praise. Then was sung in fullest chorus the song of Moses the servant of God, and of the Lamb, for he had indeed cut Rahab and sorely wounded the dragon. Sing unto the Lord, for he hath triumphed gloriously. The Lord shall reign for ever and ever, King of kings and Lord of lords.

I do not feel able, however, to describe a scene so grand, and yet so contrary to everything that flesh could discern. I choose, rather, to take my text thus: the cross is the ground of Christ's ultimate triumph, he may be said to have really triumphed there because it was by that one offering of himself that he completely vanquished all his foes, and for ever sat down at the right hand of the Majesty in the heavens. In the cross, to the spiritual eye, every victory of Christ is contained. It may not be there in fact, but it is there virtually; the germ of all our Lord's glories may be discovered by the eye of faith in the agonies of the cross.

Christ has for ever overcome all his foes, and divided the spoil upon the battlefield, and at this day he is enjoying the well-earned reward of his fearful struggle. Lift up your eyes to the great metropolis of God. The pearly gates are wide open, and the city shines with her bejewelled walls like a bride prepared for her husband. Do you see the angels crowding to the battlements? Do you observe them on every mansion of the celestial city, eagerly looking for something which has not yet arrived? At last, there is heard the sound of a trumpet, and the angels hurry to the gates – the vanguard of the redeemed host is approaching the city. Abel comes in alone, clothed in a crimson garb, the herald of the glorious army of martyrs. Hark to the shout of acclamation! This is the first of Christ's warriors, at once a soldier and a trophy. Close at his heels there follow others, who in those early times had learned the coming Saviour's fame. Behind them a mighty host may be discovered of patriarchal veterans, who have witnessed to the coming of the Lord in a wanton age. See Enoch still walking with his God, and singing sweetly – 'Behold the Lord cometh with ten thousands of his saints.' There, too, is Noah, who had sailed in the ark, with the Lord as his pilot. Then follow Abraham, Isaac, and Jacob, Moses and Joshua, and Samuel, and David, all mighty men of valour. Hearken to them as they enter! Each one of them cries, 'Unto him that loved us, and washed us from our sins in his own blood, to him be honour, and glory, and dominion, and power, for ever and ever.' Look, my brethren, with admiration upon this noble army! Mark the heroes as they march along the golden streets, everywhere meeting an enthusiastic welcome from the angels who have kept their first estate. On, on they pour, those countless legions. Was there ever such a spectacle? It is not the pageant of a day, but the 'show' of all time. For four thousand years, the army of Christ's redeemed has streamed along. Sometimes there is a short rank, for the people have been minished and brought low; but, anon, a crowd succeeds, and on, still on they come, all praising him who loved them and gave himself for them. But see, he comes! The Conqueror himself! I see his immediate herald, clad in a garment of camel's hair, wearing a leathern girdle about his loins: the Prince of the house of David is not far behind. Let every eye be open. Mark how the angels and the redeemed crowd the windows of heaven! HE comes! *He* comes! It is Jesus himself! 'Lift up your heads, O ye gates, and be ye lifted up ye everlasting doors, that the King of glory may come in.' See, he enters in the midst of acclamations. It is he! But no longer crowned with thorns. It is he! But though his hands bear the scars, they are stained with blood no longer. His eyes are as a flame of fire, and on his head are many crowns, and he hath on his vesture and on his thigh written, KING OF KINGS AND LORD OF LORDS. He stands aloft in that chariot which is 'paved with love for the daughters of Jerusalem.' Clothed in a vesture dipped in blood, he stands confessed the emperor of heaven and earth. On, on he rides, and louder than the noise of many waters and like great thunders are the acclamations which surround him! See how John's vision is become a reality, for now we can see for ourselves and hear with our own ears the new song, whereof he writes, 'They sung a new song, saying, Thou art worthy to take the book, and to open the seals thereof; for thou was slain, and has redeemed us to God by thy blood out of every kindred, and tongue, and people, and nation; and hast made us unto our God kings and priests: and we shall reign on the earth.' But who are those at his chariot wheels? Who are those grim monsters howling in the rear? I know them. First of all there is the arch enemy. Look on the old serpent bound and fettered, how he writhes his rugged length along! His azure hues all tarnished with trailing in the dust, his scales despoiled of their once-vaunted brightness. Now is the destroyer destroyed, and now shall death and hell be cast into the lake of fire. With what derision is the chief of rebels regarded! How is he become the object of everlasting contempt! He that sitteth in the heavens doth laugh, the Lord doth have him in derision. And now regard attentively yon hideous monster, Sin, chained hand in hand with his satanic sire. See how he twists and writhes in agony. Mark how he glares upon the holy city, but is unable to spit his venom there, for he is chained and gagged, and dragged along an unwilling captive at the wheels of the victor. And there, too, is Death, with his darts all broken and his hands behind him – the grim king of terrors, he, too, is a captive. Hark to the songs of the shining ones as they see these mighty prisoners dragged along! Worthy is Immanuel to sit at his Father's side, for he hath vanquished all his foes!

And now behind him I see the great mass of his people streaming in. The apostles first arrived in one goodly fellowship hymning their Lord; and then their immediate successors; and a long array of those who through cruel mockings and blood, through flame and sword, have followed their Master. These are those of whom the world was not worthy, brightest among the stars of heaven. Regard also the mighty preachers and confessors of the faith, Chrysostom, Athanasius, Augustine and the like. Witness their holy unanimity in praising their Lord. Then let your eye run along the glittering ranks till you come to the days of the Reformation. I see in the midst of the squadron, Luther, and Calvin, and Zwingle, three holy brothers. I see just before them Wickliffe, and Huss, and Jerome of Prague, all marching together, and then I see a number that no man can number, converted to God through these earliest reformers, and those who followed them. Looking down to our own time I see the stream broaden and widen, for many are the soldiers who have in these last times entered into their Master's triumph. We may mourn their absence from *us,* but we must rejoice in their presence with the *Lord.* But what is the unanimous shout which rolls along from the first rank to the last? It is this: 'Unto him that loved us, and washed us from our sins in his own blood, to him be glory and dominion for ever and ever!'

I have no time to enlarge further, or else I might describe the glorious pictures at the end of the procession; for in the old Roman triumphs, the deeds of the conqueror were all depicted in paintings. The towns he had taken, the rivers he had passed, the provinces he had subdued, the battles he had fought, were represented upon tablets and exposed to the view of the people, who with great festivity and rejoicing accompanied him in throngs, or beheld him from the windows of their houses, and filled the air with their applause. I might present to you first of all a picture of hell's dungeons blown to atoms. Satan had prepared deep in the depths of darkness a prison-house for God's elect; but Christ has not left one stone upon another. I see the chains broken, and the prison doors burnt with fire. On one picture I see heaven open to all believers, and on another the grave despoiled. But we cannot stay to describe the records of his love. We know that the time shall come when the triumphant procession shall cease, when the last of his redeemed shall have entered into the city, and when he shall deliver up the kingdom to God, even the Father, and God shall be all in all.

Say, my soul, wilt thou have a humble part in that glorious pageant? Wilt thou follow as one of his chosen soldiery? Wilt thou join in the thundering hosanna? Shall thy voice help to swell the everlasting chorus? Sometimes, I fear it shall not. There are times when the awful question comes – what if my name should be left out when he shall read the muster-roll? Brethren, does not that thought trouble *you*? Never rest till the question is decided once for all. I put the inquiry again. Can you answer it? Will you be there with him? Will you behold him triumph over sin, death and hell at the last? Can you answer this question? There is another, but the answer will serve

for both – dost thou believe on the Lord Jesus Christ?
Is he thy confidence and thy trust? Hast thou committed thy soul to his keeping? Reposing on his sacrifice
canst thou say for thine immortal spirit,

> 'Other refuge have I none,
>   Hangs my helpless soul on thee?'

If thou canst say that, thine eyes shall see him in the
day of his glory, and thou shalt sit with him upon his
throne, even as he has overcome and sits down with
his Father upon his throne.

CHRIST
THE DESTROYER OF DEATH

'The last enemy that shall be destroyed is death.'
– 1 Corinthians 15:26

In the five previous discourses we have been following
our Lord and Master through his great achievements:
we have seen him as the End of the Law, as the
Conqueror of Satan, as the Overcomer of the World,
as the Creator of All Things New, and as the Spoiler
of Principalities and Powers, and now we behold him
as the Destroyer of Death. In this and in all his other
glorious deeds let us adore him.

May the Spirit of God lead us into the full meaning
of this, which is one of the Redeemer's grandest
characters.

How wonderfully is our Lord Jesus *one with man!*
For when the Psalmist David had considered 'the
heavens, the work of God's fingers,' he said, 'Lord,
what is man, that thou art mindful of him? And the
son of man, that thou visitest him?' He was speaking
of Christ. You would have thought he was thinking of
man in his humblest estate, and that he was wondering
that God should be pleased to honour so frail a being
as the poor fallen son of Adam. You would never have
dreamed that the glorious gospel lay hid within those
words of grateful adoration. Yet in the course of that
meditation David went on to say, 'Thou madest him
to have dominion over the works of thy hands; thou
hast put all things under his feet.' Now, had it not
been for the interpretation of the Holy Spirit, we
should still have considered that he was speaking of
men in general, and of man's natural dominion over
the brute creation; but, behold, while that is true,
there is another and a far more important truth

concealed within it; for David, as a prophet, was all the while chiefly speaking of the man of men, the model man, the second Adam, the head of the new race of men. It was of Jesus, the Son of man, as honoured of the Father, that the psalmist sang, 'He hath put all things under his feet.' Strange, was it not, that when he spake of man he must of necessity speak also of our Lord? And yet, when we consider the thing, it is but natural and according to truth, and only remarkable to us because in our minds we too often consider Jesus and man as far removed, and too little regard him as truly one with man.

Now, see how the apostle infers from the psalm the necessity of the resurrection, for if all things must be put under the feet of the man Christ Jesus, then every form of evil must be conquered by him, and death among the rest. 'He must reign till he hath put all enemies under his feet.' It must be so, and therefore death itself must ultimately be overcome. Thus, out of that simple sentence in the psalm, which we should have read far otherwise without the light of the Holy Spirit, the apostle gathereth the doctrine of the resurrection. The Holy Spirit taught his servant Paul how by a subtle chemistry he could distil from simple words a precious fragrant essence, which the common reader never suspected to be there. Texts have their secret drawers, their box within a box, their hidden souls which lie asleep till he who placed them on their secret couches awakens them that they may speak to the hearts of his chosen. Could you ever have guessed resurrection from the eighth Psalm? No, nor could you have believed, had it not been told you, that there is fire in the flint, oil in the rock, and bread in the earth we tread upon. Man's books have usually far less in them than we expect, but the book of the Lord is full of surprises, it is a mass of light, a mountain of priceless revelations. We little know what yet lies hidden within the Scriptures. We know the form of sound words as the Lord has taught it to us, and by it we will abide, but there are inner storehouses into which we have not peered; chambers of revelation lit up with bright lamps, perhaps too bright for our eyes at this present. If Paul, when the Spirit of God rested upon him, could see so much in the songs of David, the day may come when we also shall see still more in the epistles of Paul, and wonder at ourselves that we did not understand better the things which the Holy Ghost has so freely spoken to us by the apostle. May we at this time be enabled to look deep and far, and behold the sublime glories of our risen Lord. To the text itself then: *death is an enemy: death is an enemy to be destroyed: death is an enemy to be destroyed last:* – 'the last enemy that shall be destroyed is death.'

1. DEATH AN ENEMY. *It was so born,* even as Haman the Agagite was the enemy of Israel by his descent. Death is the child of our direct foe, for 'sin when it is finished bringeth forth death.' 'Sin entered into the world and death by sin.' Now, that which is distinctly the fruit of transgression cannot be other than an enemy of man. Death was introduced into the world on that gloomy day which saw our fall, and he that had the power of it is our arch enemy and betrayer, the devil: from both of which facts we must regard it as the manifest enemy of man. Death is an alien in this world, it did not enter into the original design of the unfallen creation, but its intrusion mars and spoils the whole. It is no part of the Great Shepherd's flock, but it is a wolf which cometh to kill and to destroy. Geology tells us that there was death among the various forms of life from the first ages of the globe's history, even when as yet the world was not fitted up as the dwelling of man. This I can believe and

still regard death as the result of sin. If it can be proved that there is such an organic unity between man and the lower animals that they would not have died if Adam had not sinned, then I see in those deaths before Adam the antecedent consequences of a sin which was then uncommitted. If by the merits of Jesus there was salvation before he had offered his atoning sacrifice, I do not find it hard to conceive that the foreseen demerits of sin may have cast the shadow of death over the ages which preceded man's transgression. Of that we do not know much, nor is it important that we should; but certain is it that as far as this present creation is concerned death is not God's invited guest, but an intruder whose presence mars the feast. Man in his folly welcomed Satan and sin when they forced their way into the high festival of Paradise, but he never welcomed death: even his blind eyes could see in that skeleton form a cruel foe. As the lion to the herds of the plain, as the scythe to the flowers of the field, as the wind to the sere leaves of the forest, such is death to the sons of men; and they fear it by an inward instinct because their conscience tells them that it is the child of their sin.

Death is well called an enemy, *for it does an enemy's* work towards us. For what purpose doth an enemy come but to root up, and to pull down, and to destroy? Death tears in pieces that comely handiwork of God, the fabric of the human body, so marvellously wrought by the fingers of divine skill. Casting this rich embroidery into the grave among the armies of the worm, to its fierce soldiery death divideth 'to every one a prey of divers colours, of divers colours of needlework;' and they ruthlessly rend in pieces the spoil. This building of our manhood is a house fair to look upon, but death the destroyer darkens its windows, shakes its pillars, closes its doors and causes the sound of the grinding to cease. Then the daughters of music are brought low, and the strong men bow themselves. This Vandal spares no work of life, however full of wisdom, or beauty, for it looseth the silver cord and breaketh the golden bowl. Lo, at the fountain the costly pitcher is utterly broken, and at the cistern the well-wrought wheel is dashed in pieces. Death is a fierce invader of the realms of life, and where it comes it fells every good tree, stops all wells of water, and mars evey good piece of land with stones. See you a man when death has wrought his will upon him, what a ruin he is! How is his beauty turned to ashes, and his comeliness to corruption. Surely an enemy hath done this.

Look, my brethren, at the course of death throughout all ages and in all lands. What field is there without its grave? What city without its cemetery? What family without its burial-place? As the sandy shore is covered with the upcastings of the worm, so art thou, O earth, covered with those grass-grown hillocks beneath which sleep the departed generations of men. And thou, O sea, even thou, art not without thy dead! as if the earth were all too full of corpses and they jostled each other in their crowded sepulchres, even into thy caverns, O mighty main, the bodies of the dead are cast. Thy waves must become defiled with the carcases of men, and on thy floor must lie the bones of the slain! Our enemy, death, has marched as it were with sword and fire ravaging the human race. Neither Goth, nor Hun, nor Tartar could have slain so universally all that breathed, for death has suffered none to escape. Everywhere it has withered household joys and created sorrow and sighing; in all lands where the sun is seen it hath blinded men's eyes with weeping. The tear of the bereaved, the wail of the widow, and the moan of the orphan – these have been death's war music, and he has found therein a song of victory.

The greatest conquerors have only been death's slaughtermen, journeymen butchers working in his shambles. War is nothing better than death holding carnival, and devouring his prey a little more in haste than is his common wont.

Death has done the work of an enemy to those of us who have as yet escaped his arrows. Those who have lately stood around a new-made grave and buried half their hearts can tell you what an enemy death is. It takes the friend from our side, and the child from our bosom, neither does it care for our crying. He has fallen who was the pillar of the household; she has been snatched away who was the brightness of the hearth. The little one is torn out of its mother's bosom though its loss almost breaks her heartstrings; and the blooming youth is taken from his father's side though the parent's fondest hopes are thereby crushed. Death has no pity for the young and no mercy for the old; he pays no regard to the good or to the beautiful. His scythe cuts down sweet flowers and noxious weeds with equal readiness. He cometh into our garden, trampleth down our lilies and scattereth our roses on the ground; yea, and even the most modest flowers planted in the corner, and hiding their beauty beneath the leaves that they may blush unseen, death spieth out even these, and cares nothing for their fragrance, but withers them with his burning breath. He is thine enemy indeed, thou fatherless child, left for the pitiless storm of a cruel world to beat upon, with none to shelter thee. He is thine enemy, O widow, for the light of thy life is gone, and the desire of thine eyes has been removed with a stroke. He is thine enemy, husband, for thy house is desolate and thy little children cry for their mother of whom death has robbed thee.

He is the enemy of us all, for what head of a family

among us has not had to say to him, 'Me thou has bereaved again and again!' Especially is death an enemy to the living when he invades God's house and causes the prophet and the priest to be numbered with the dead. The church mourns when her most useful ministers are smitten down, when the watchful eye is closed in darkness, and the instructive tongue is mute. Yet how often does death thus war against us! The earnest, the active, the indefatigable are taken away. Those mightiest in prayer, those most affectionate in heart, those most exemplary in life, those are cut down in the midst of their labours, leaving behind them a church which needs them more than tongue can tell. If the Lord does but threaten to permit death to seize a beloved pastor, the souls of his people are full of grief, and they view death as their worst foe, while they plead with the Lord and entreat him to bid their minister live.

Even those who die may well count death to be their enemy: I mean not now that they have risen to their thrones, and, as disembodied spirits, behold the King in his beauty, but aforetime while death was approaching them. He seemed to their trembling flesh to be a foe, for it is not in nature, except in moments of extreme pain or aberration of mind, or of excessive expectation of glory, for us to be in love with death. It was wise of our Creator so to constitute us that the soul loves the body and the body loves the soul, and they desire to dwell together as long as they may, else had there been no care for self-preservation, and suicide would have destroyed the race.

'For who would bear the whips and scorns of
  time,
 The oppressor's wrong, the proud man's
  contumely,
When he himself might his quietus make
 With a bare bodkin?'

It is a first law of our nature that skin for skin, yea, all
that a man hath will he give for his life, and thus we
are nerved to struggle for existence, and to avoid that
which would destroy us. This useful instinct renders
death an enemy, but it also aids in keeping us from
that crime of all crimes the most sure of damnation if a
man commit wilfully and in his sound mind; I mean
the crime of self-murder.

When death cometh even to the good man he
cometh as an enemy, for he is attended by such terrible
heralds and grim outriders as do greatly scare us. The
poet's list reads like a roll written within and without
with lamentations.

'Fever with brow of fire;
 Consumption wan; palsy, half-warmed
  with life,
 And half a clay-cold lump; joint-torturing gout,
  And ever-gnawing rheum; convulsion wild;
 Swoln dropsy; panting asthma; apoplex
  Full gorged.'

These add terrors to the aspect of death. He comes
with pains and griefs, with sighs and tears. Clouds and
darkness are round about him, an atmosphere laden
with dust oppresses those whom he approaches, and a
cold wind chills them even to the marrow. He rides on
the pale horse and by the tramp of that terrible steed
the worm is awakened to gnaw the slain. When we

forget other grand truths and only remember those dreadful things, death is the king of terrors to us. Hearts are sickened and reins are loosened because of him.

But, indeed, he is an enemy, for what comes he to do to our body? I know he doeth that which ultimately leadeth to its betterness, but still it is that which in itself, and for the present, is not joyous, but grievous. He comes to take the light from the eyes, the hearing from the ears, the speech from the tongue, the activity from the hand, and the thought from the brain. He comes to transform a living man into a mass of putrefaction, to degrade the beloved form of brother and friend to such a condition of corruption that affection itself cries out, 'Bury my dead out of my sight.' Death, thou child of sin, Christ hath transformed thee marvellously, but in thyself thou art an enemy before whom flesh and blood tremble, for they know that thou art the murderer of all of woman born, whose thirst for human prey the blood of nations cannot slake.

If you think for a few moments of this enemy, you will observe some of his points of character. He is the *common* foe of all God's people, and the enemy of all men; for however some have been persuaded that they should not die, yet is there no discharge in this war; and if in this conscription a man escapes the ballot many and many a year till his grey beard seems to defy the winter's hardest frost, yet must the man of iron yield at last. It is appointed unto all men once to die. The strongest man has no elixir of eternal life wherewith to renew his youth amid the decays of age: nor has the wealthiest prince a price wherewith to bribe destruction. To the grave must thou descend, O crowned monarch, for sceptres and shovels are akin. To the sepulchre must thou go down, O mighty man of valour, for sword and spade are of like metal. The prince is brother to the worm, and must dwell in the same house. Of our whole race it is true, 'Dust thou art, and unto dust shalt thou return.'

Death is also a *subtle* foe, lurking everywhere, even in the most harmless things. Who can tell where death has not prepared his ambuscades? He meets us both at home and abroad; at the table he assails men in their food, and at the fountain he poisons their drink. He waylayeth us in the streets, and he seizeth us in our beds; he rideth on the storm at sea, and he walks with us when we are on our way upon the solid land. Whither can we fly to escape from thee, O death, for from the summit of the Alps men have fallen to their graves, and in the deep places of the earth where the miner goeth down to find the precious ore, there hast thou sacrificed many a hecatomb of precious lives. Death is a subtle foe, and with noiseless footfalls follows close at our heels when least we think of him.

He is an enemy whom *none of us will be able to avoid,* take what by-paths we may, nor can we escape from him when our hour is come. Into this fowler's nets, like the birds, we shall all fly; in his great *seine* must all the fishes of the great sea of life be taken when their day is come. As surely as sets the sun, or as the midnight stars at length descend beneath the horizon, or as the waves sink back into the sea, or as the bubble bursts, so must we all early or late come to our end, and disappear from earth to be known no more among the living.

Sudden too, full often, are the assaults of this enemy.

'Leaves have their time to fall,
  And flowers to wither at the north wind's
    breath,
And stars to set – but all
  Thou has all seasons for thine own, O
    Death!'

Such things have happened as for men to die without an instant's notice; with a psalm upon their lips they have passed away, or engaged in their daily business they have been summoned to give in their account. We have heard of one who, when the morning paper brought him news that a friend in business had died, was drawing on his boots to go to his counting-house, and observed with a laugh, that as far as he was concerned, he was so busy he had no time to die. Yet, ere the words were finished, he fell forward and was a corpse. Sudden deaths are not so uncommon as to be marvels if we dwell in the centre of a large circle of mankind. Thus is death a foe not to be despised or trifled with. Let us remember all his characteristics, and we shall not be inclined to think lightly of the grim enemy whom our glorious Redeemer has destroyed.

2. Secondly, let us remember that death is AN ENEMY TO BE DESTROYED. Remember that our Lord Jesus Christ has already wrought a great victory upon death, so that he has delivered us from lifelong bondage through its fear. He has not yet *destroyed death,* but he has gone very near to it, for we are told that he has 'abolished death and hath brought life and immortality to light through the gospel.' This surely must come very near to having destroyed death altogether.

In the first place, our Lord has subdued death in the very worst sense by having delivered his people from spiritual death. 'And you hath he quickened, who were dead in trespasses and sins.' Once you had no divine life whatever, but the death of original depravity remained upon you, and so you were dead to all divine and spiritual things; but now, beloved, the Spirit of God, even he that raised up Jesus Christ from the dead, has raised you up into newness of life, and you have become new creatures in Christ Jesus. In this sense death has been subdued.

Our Lord in his lifetime also conquered death by restoring certain individuals to life. There were three memorable cases in which at his bidding the last enemy resigned his prey. Our Lord went into the ruler's house and saw the little girl who had lately fallen asleep in death, around whom they wept and lamented: he heard their scornful laughter, when he said, 'She is not dead, but sleepeth,' and he put them all out and said to her, 'Maid, arise.' Then was the spoiler spoiled, and the dungeon door set open. He stopped the funeral procession at the gates of Nain, whence they were carrying forth a young man, 'the only son of his mother, and she was a widow,' and he said, 'Young man, I say unto thee, arise.' When that young man sat up and our Lord delivered him to his mother, then again was the prey taken from the mighty. Chief of all, when Lazarus had laid in the grave so long that his sister said, 'Lord, by this time he stinketh;' when, in obedience to the word, 'Lazarus, come forth!' forth came the raised one with his grave-clothes still about him, but yet really quickened, then was death seen to be subservient to the Son of Man. 'Loose him and let him go,' said the conquering Christ, and death's bonds were removed, for the lawful captive was delivered. When at the Redeemer's resurrection many of the saints arose and came out of their graves into the holy city, then was the crucified Lord proclaimed to be victorious over death and the grave.

Still, brethren, these were but preliminary skir-mishes and mere foreshadowings of the grand victory by which death was overthrown. *The real triumph was achieved upon the cross:*

> 'He hell in hell laid low;
>   Made sin, he sin o'erthrew;
>   Bow'd to the grave, destroy'd it so,
>   And death, by dying, slew.'

When Christ died he suffered the penalty of death on the behalf of all his people, and therefore no believer now dies by way of punishment for sin, since we cannot dream that a righteous God would twice exact the penalty for one offence. Death since Jesus died is not a penal infliction upon the children of God: as such he has abolished it, and it can never be enforced. Why die the saints then? Why, because their bodies must be changed ere they can enter heaven. 'Flesh and blood' as they are 'cannot inherit the king-dom of God.' A divine change must take place upon the body before it will be fit for incorruption and glory; and death and the grave are, as it were, the refining pot and the furnace by means of which the body is made ready for its future bliss. Death, it is true thou art not yet destroyed, but our living Redeemer has so changed thee that thou art no longer death, but something other than thy name! Saints die not now, but they are dissolved and depart. Death is the loosing of the cable that the bark may freely sail to the fair havens. Death is the fiery chariot in which we ascend to God; it is the gentle voice of the Great King, who cometh into his banqueting hall, and saith, 'Friend, come up higher.' Behold, on eagles' wings we mount, we fly, far from this land of mist and cloud, into the eternal serenity and brilliance of God's own house above. Yes, our Lord has abolished death. The sting of death is sin, and our great Substitute has taken that sting away by his great sacrifice. Stingless, death abides among the people of God, but it so little harms them that to them 'it is not death to die.'

Further, Christ vanquished death and thoroughly overcame him when he rose. What a temptation one has to paint a picture of the resurrection, but I will not be led aside to attempt more than a few touches. When our great Champion awoke from his brief sleep of death and found himself in the withdrawing-room of the grave, he quietly proceeded to put off the garments of the tomb. How leisurely he proceeded! He folded up the napkin and placed it by itself, that those who lose their friends might wipe their eyes therewith; and then he took off the winding sheet and laid the graveclothes by themselves that they might be there when his saints come thither, so that the chamber might be well furnished, and the bed ready sheeted and prepared for their rest. The sepulchre is no longer an empty vault, a dreary charnel, but a chamber of rest, a dormitory furnished and prepared, hung with the arras which Christ himself has bequeathed. It is now no more a damp, dark, dreary prison: Jesus has changed all that.

''Tis now a cell where angels use
To come and go with heavenly news.'

The angel from heaven rolled away the stone from our Lord's sepulchre and let in the fresh air and light again upon our Lord, and he stepped out more than a conqueror. Death had fled. The grave had capitulated.

117

'Lives again our glorious King!
'Where, O death, is now they sting?'
Once he died our souls to save;
'Where's thy victory, boasting grave?'

Well, brethren, as surely as Christ rose, so did he
guarantee as an absolute certainty the resurrection
of all his saints into a glorious life for their bodies,
the life of their souls never having paused even for a
moment. In this he conquered death; and since that
memorable victory, every day Christ is overcoming
death, for he gives his Spirit to his saints, and having
that Spirit within them they meet the last enemy
without alarm: often they confront him with songs,
perhaps more frequently they face him with calm
countenance, and fall asleep with peace. I will not fear
thee, death, why should I? Thou lookest like a dragon,
but thy sting is gone. They teeth are broken, O old
lion, wherefore should I fear thee? I know thou art no
more able to destroy me, but thou art sent as a
messenger to conduct me to the golden gate wherein I
shall enter and see my Saviour's unveiled face for ever.
Expiring saints have often said that their last beds
have been the best they have ever slept upon. Many of
them have enquired,

'Tell me, my soul, can this be death?'

To die has been so different a thing from what they
expected it to be, so lightsome, and so joyous; they
have been so unloaded of all care, have felt so relieved
instead of burdened, that they have wondered whether
this could be the monster they had been so afraid of all
their days. They find it a pin's prick, whereas they
feared it would prove a sword-thrust: it is the shutting
of the eye on earth and the opening of it in heaven,

whereas they thought it would have been a stretching upon the rack, or a dreary passage through a dismal region of gloom and dread. Beloved, our exalted Lord has overcome death in all these ways.

But now, observe, that this is not the text: – the text speaks of something yet to be done. 'The last enemy that *shall be* destroyed is death,' so that death in the sense meant by the text is not destroyed yet. He is to be destroyed, and how will that be?

Well, I take it, death will be destroyed first, in the sense that, at the coming of Christ, *those who are alive and remain shall not see death.* They shall be changed; there must be a change even to those who are then living before they can inherit eternal life, but they shall not actually die. Do not envy them, for they will have no preference beyond those that sleep; rather do I think theirs to be the inferior lot of the two in some respects. But they will not know death: the multitude of the Lord's own who will be alive at his coming will pass into the glory without needing to die. Thus death, as far as they are concerned, will be destroyed.

But the sleeping ones, the myriads who have left their flesh and bones to moulder back to earth, death shall be destroyed even as to them, for when the trumpet sounds they shall rise from the tomb. *The resurrection is the destruction of death.* We never taught, nor believed, nor thought that every particle of every body that was put into the grave would come to its fellow, and that the absolutely identical material would rise; but we do say that the identical body will be raised, and that as surely as there cometh out of the ground the seed that was put into it, though in very different guise, for it cometh not forth as a seed but as a flower, so surely shall the same body rise again. The same material is not necessary, but there shall come out of the grave, ay, come out of the earth, if it never saw a grave, or come out of the sea if devoured by monsters, that selfsame body for true identity which was inhabited by the soul while here below. Was it not so with our Lord? Even so shall it be with his own people, and then shall be brought to pass the saying that is written, 'Death is swallowed up in victory. O death, where is thy sting? O grave, where is thy victory?'

There will be this feature in our Lord's victory, that death will be fully destroyed because *those who rise will not be one whit the worse for having died.* I believe concerning those new bodies that there will be no trace upon them of the feebleness of old age, none of the marks of long and wearying sickness, none of the scars of martyrdom. Death shall not have left his mark upon them at all, except it be some glory spot which shall be to their honour, like the scars in the flesh of the Wellbeloved, which are his chief beauty even now in the eyes of those for whom his hands and feet were pierced. In this sense death shall be destroyed, because he shall have done no damage to the saints at all, the very trace of decay shall have been swept away from the redeemed.

And then, finally, *there shall, after this triumph of the Lord, be no more death,* neither sorrow, nor crying, for the former things have passed away. 'Christ being raised from the dead dieth no more, death hath no more dominion over him;' and so also the quickened ones, his own redeemed, they, too, shall die no more. Oh dreadful, dreadful supposition, that they should ever have to undergo temptation or pain, or death a second time. It cannot be. 'Because I live,' says Christ, 'ye shall live also.' Yet the doctrine of the natural immortality of the soul having been given up by some, certain of them have felt obliged to give up with the eternity of future punishment the eternity of future bliss, and assuredly as far as some great proof-texts are concerned, they stand or fall together. 'These shall go away into everlasting punishment, and the righteous into life eternal;' if the one state be short, so must the other be: whatever the adjective means in the one case it means in the other. To us the word means endless duration in both cases, and we look forward to a bliss which shall never know an end. Then, in the tearless, sorrowless, graveless country, death shall be utterly destroyed.

3. And now last of all, and the word 'last' sounds fitly in this case, DEATH IS TO BE DESTROYED LAST. Because he came in last he must go out last. Death was not the first of our foes: first came the devil, then sin, then death. Death is not the worst of enemies; death is an enemy, but he is much to be preferred to our other adversaries. It were better to die a thousand times than to sin. To be tried by death is nothing compared with being tempted by the devil. The mere physical pains connected with dissolution are comparative trifles compared with the hideous grief which is caused by sin and the burden which a sense of guilt casts upon the soul. No, death is but a secondary mischief compared with the defilement of sin. Let the great enemies go down first; smite the shepherd and the sheep will be scattered; let sin, and Satan, the lord of all these evils, be smitten first, and death may well be left to the last.

Notice, that death is the last enemy to each individual Christian and the last to be destroyed. Well now, if the word of God says it is the last, I want to remind you of a little piece of practical wisdom – leave him to be the last. Brother, do not dispute the appointed order, but let the last be last. I have known a brother wanting to vanquish death long before he died. But, brother, you do not want dying grace till dying moments. What would be the good of dying grace while you are yet alive? A boat will only be needful when you reach a river. Ask for living grace, and glorify Christ thereby, and then you shall have dying grace when dying time comes. Your enemy is going to be destroyed, but not today. There is a great host of enemies to be fought today, and you may be content to let this one alone for a while. This enemy will be destroyed, but of the times and the seasons we are in ignorance; our wisdom is to be good soldiers of Jesus Christ as the duty of every day requires. Take your trials as they come, brother! As the enemies march up slay them, rank upon rank; but if you fail in the name of God to smite the front ranks, and say, 'No, I am only careful to prepare for the assault of the rear rank,' then you are playing the fool. Leave the final shock of arms till the last adversary advances, and meanwhile hold you your place in the conflict. God will in due time help you to overcome your last enemy, but meanwhile see to it that you overcome the world, the flesh, and the devil. If you live well you will die well. That same covenant in which the Lord Jesus gave you life contains also the grant of death, for 'All things are yours whether things present or things to come, or life or death, all are yours, and ye are Christ's, and Christ is God's.'

Why is death left to the last? Well, I think it is because Christ can make much use of him. The last enemy that shall be destroyed is death, because death is of great service before he is destroyed. Oh, what lessons some of us have learned from death! 'Our dying friends come o'er us like a cloud to damp our brainless ardours,' to make us feel that these poor fleeting toys are not worth living for; that as others pass away so must we also be gone, and thus they help to make us set loose by this world, and urge us to take wing and mount towards the world to come. There are, perhaps, no sermons like the deaths which have happened in our households; the departures of our beloved friends have been to us solemn discourses of divine wisdom, which our heart could not help hearing. So Christ has spared death to make him a preacher to his saints.

And you know, brethren, that if there had been no death the saints of God would not have had the opportunity to exhibit the highest ardour of their love. Where has love to Christ triumphed most? Why, in the death of the martyrs at the stake and on the rack. O Christ, thou never hadst such garlands woven for thee by human hands as they have brought thee who have come up to heaven from the forests of persecution, having waded through streams of blood. By death for Christ the saints have glorified him most.

So is it in their measure with saints who die from ordinary deaths; they would have had no such test for faith and work for patience as they now have if there had been no death. Part of the reason of the continuance of this dispensation is that the Christ of God may be glorified, but if believers never died, the supreme consummation of faith's victory must have been unknown. Brethren, if I may die as I have seen some of our church members die, I court the grand occasion. I would not wish to escape death by some by-road if I may sing as they sang. If I may have such hosannas and hallelujahs beaming in my very eyes as I have seen as well as heard from them, it were a blessed thing to die. Yes, as a supreme test of love and faith, death is well respited a while to let the saints glorify their Master.

Besides, brethren, without death we should not be so conformed to Christ as we shall be if we fall asleep in him. If there could be any jealousies in heaven among the saints, I think that any saint who does not die, but is changed when Christ comes, could almost meet me and you, who probably will die, and say, 'My brother, there is one thing I have missed, I never lay in the grave, I never had the chill hand of death laid on me, and so in that I was not conformed to my Lord. But *you* know what it is to have fellowship with him, even in his death.' Did I not well say that they that were alive and remain should have no preference over them that are asleep? I think the preference, if there be any, shall belong to us who sleep in Jesus, and wake up in his likeness.

Death, beloved, is not yet destroyed, because he brings the saints home. He does but come to them and whisper his message, and in a moment they are supremely blessed,

> 'Have done with sin and care and woe,
>   And with the Saviour rest.'

And so death is not destroyed yet, for he answers useful purposes.

But, beloved, he is going to be destroyed. He is the last enemy of the church collectively. The church as a body has had a mass of foes to contend with, but after the resurrection we shall say, 'This is the last enemy. Not another foe is left.' Eternity shall roll on in ceaseless bliss. There may be changes, bringing new delights; perhaps in the eternity to come there may be eras and ages of yet more amazing bliss, and still more superlative ecstasy; but there shall be

> 'No rude alarm of raging foes,
>   No cares to break the long repose.'

The last enemy that shall be destroyed is death, and if

the last be slain there can be no future foe. The battle is fought and the victory is won for ever. And who hath won it? Who but the Lamb that sitteth on the throne, to whom let us all ascribe honour, and glory, and majesty, and power, and dominion, and might, for ever and ever. The Lord help us in our solemn adoration. Amen.

CHRIST
THE SEEKER AND SAVIOUR
OF THE LOST

'For the Son of man is come to seek and to save that which was lost.' – Luke 19:10

We have now considered six of the glorious achievements of our divine Lord and Saviour, and it is time to conclude the series. How shall we crown the edifice? The best wine should be kept unto the last, but where shall we find it? The choice is wide, but amid so many wonders which shall we select? What shall be the seventh great work concerning which we shall extol him? Many marvels suggested themselves to me and each one was, assuredly, worthy to occupy the place; but as I could not take all, I resolved to close with one of the simplest and most practical. *His saving sinners* seemed to me to be practically the chief of all his works, for it was for this purpose that the rest of his achievements were attempted and performed. Had it not been for the salvation of men, I know not that we had ever known our Lord as the destroyer of death or the overcomer of Satan; and, certainly, if he had not saved the lost, I am unable to perceive what glory there would have been in the overcoming of the world, or in the creation of all things new. The salvation of men was the prize of his life's race; for this he girded up his loins and distanced every adversary. The salvation of the lost was the joy which was set before him, for the sake of which he 'endured the cross, despising the shame.' Although it seems, at first sight, that in selecting our present topic we have descended from the transcendent glories of our champion to more common things, it is not indeed so. The victories of our Lord which are written in the book of the wars of the Lord, when he led captivity captive and robbed death of his sting, may strike us as more astounding, but yet in very truth this is the summing-up of his great works; this is the issue, the flower, and crown of all. 'The Son of man is come to seek and to save that which was lost,' is a sentence as majestic as prophet ever penned when in fullest inspiration he extolled the Prince of Peace.

1. Notice, first, OUR LORD'S GRACIOUS MISSION. *'The Son of man is come.'* When he was here among men, he could use the present tense, and say 'is come.' That was an improvement upon what prophets had to say, for they only spoke of him as the coming one – as one who in the fulness of time would be manifested. The promise was amazing, but what shall I say of the actual performance when the Word made flesh could say, 'The Son of man is come.' To us, today, the coming of Christ to seek and to save the lost is an accomplished fact, a matter of history, most sure and certain. And what a fact it is! You have often thought of it, but have you ever worked your mind into the very heart of it – that God has actually visited this world in human form – that he before whom angels bow has actually been here, in fashion like ourselves, feeding the hungry crowds of Palestine, healing their sick, and raising their dead? I know not what may be the peculiar boast of other planets, but this poor star cannot be excelled, for on this world the Creator has stood. This earth has been trodden by the feet of God, and yet it was not crushed beneath the mighty burden, because he deigned to link his Deity with our humanity. The incarnation is a wonder of wonders, but it does not belong to the realm of imagination, or even of expectation, for it has actually been beheld by mortal eyes. We claim your faith for a

fact which has really taken place. If we asked you by faith to expect a marvel yet to come, we trust the Spirit of God would enable you so to do, that, like Abraham, you might foresee the blessing and be glad. But the miracle of miracles has been wrought. The Son of the Highest *has been* here. From Bethlehem to Calvary he has traversed life's pilgrimage. Thirty years or more yonder canopy of sky hung above the head of Deity in human form. O wondrous joy! Say rather, O matchless hive of perfect sweets, for a thousand joys lie close compacted in the word 'Immanuel' – God with us. 'The Son of man *is* come.'

> 'Welcome to our wondering sight,
>   Eternity within a span!
> Summer in winter! Day in night!
>   Heaven in earth! And God in man!
> Great Little One, whose glorious birth
>   Lifts earth to heaven, stoops heaven to earth.'

Our Lord had come upon his sacred mission as soon as he was really the Son of man, for aforetime he was known only as the Son of God. Others had borne the name of 'son of man,' but none deserved it so well as he. Ezekiel, for reasons which we need not now stay to consider, is called 'son of man' a very large number of times. Perhaps, like John in Christ's own day, Ezekiel had much of the spirit and character which were manifest in our Lord, and so the name was the more suitable to him. Certainly he had Christ's eagle eye, and Christ's spiritual nature, and was filled with light and knowledge, and so, as if to remind him that he who is like his Lord in excellence must also have fellowship with him in lowliness, he is again and again reminded that he is still 'the son of man.' When our Lord came into this world, he seemed to select that title of 'Son of man' to himself, and make it his own special name; and worthily so, for other men are the sons of this man or that, but his is no restricted humanity, it is manhood of the universal type. Jesus is not born into the race of the Jews so much as into the human family. He is not to be claimed for any age, place, or nationality – he is the 'Son of man.' And this, I say, is how he comes to man; so that as long as Christ is the Son of man, we may still say of him that he comes to seek and to save the lost. I know that in person he has gone back to heaven; I know that the cloud has received him out of our sight; but the very taking upon himself of our humanity was a coming down to seek and save the lost, and as he has not laid that humanity aside, he is still with men, continuing to seek and save: even to this day 'he is able to save to the uttermost them that come unto God by him, seeing he ever liveth to make intercession for them.' So that if I treat the text as if Jesus were among us still, I shall not err, for he is here in the sense of seeking the same end, though it is by his Spirit and by his servants rather than by his own bodily presence. He has said, 'Lo, I am with you alway, even to the end of the world,' and that saying is found in connection with the agency which he has established for seeking and saving lost men, by making men disciples and teaching them the way of life. As long as this dispensation lasts, it will still be true that the great Saviour and friend of man has come among us and is seeking and saving the lost.

2. Now secondly, let us see HIS MAIN INTENT IN COMING HERE BELOW. 'The Son of man is come *to seek and to save that which was lost.*' The intent breaks itself up into two points – the persons, the lost; and the purpose – the seeking and the saving of them.

Christ's main intent in coming here bore upon *the lost*. Proud men do not like us to preach this truth. It was but yesterday that I saw it alleged against Christianity that it discourages virtue and patronizes the guilty. They say that we ministers lift the sinful into the most prominent place and give them the preference above the moral and excellent in our preaching. This is a soft impeachment to which, in a better sense than is intended by those who bring it, we are glad to plead guilty. We may well be excused if our preaching seeks the lost, for these are the persons whom our Lord has come to seek and to save. The main stress and intent of the incarnation of God in the person of Christ lies with the guilty, the fallen, the unworthy, the lost. His errand of mercy has nothing to do with those who are good and righteous in themselves, if such there be; but it has to do with sinners, real sinners, guilty not of nominal but of actual sins, and who have gone so far therein as to be lost. Wherefore cavil ye at this? Why should he come to seek and to save that which is not lost? Should the shepherd seek the sheep which has not gone astray? Answer me. Wherefore should he come to be the Physician of those who are not sick? Should he light a candle and sweep the house to look for pieces of money which are not lost but lie bright and untarnished in his hand? To what purpose would this be? Would you have him paint the lily and gild refined gold? Would you make him a mere busybody, offering superfluous aid? With those who think themselves pure what hath the cleansing blood of Jesus to do? Is a Saviour a needless person, and was his work a needless business? It must be so if it be intended for those who want it not.

Who want a Saviour most? Answer ye this. Should not mercy exercise itself where there is most need for it? This world is like a battlefield, over which the fierce hurricane of conflict has swept, and the surgeons have come to deal with those who lie upon its plains. To whom shall they go first? Shall they not turn first to those who are most terribly wounded, and who are bleeding almost to the death? Will you quarrel with us if we declare that the first to be taken to the hospital should be those who are in the direst need? Will you be angry if we say that the liniment is for the wounded? That the bandages are for the broken limbs and that the medicine is for the sick? A strange quarrel this would be. If ever it should begin, a fool must begin it, for no wise man would ever raise the question. Blessed Christ of God, we will not cavil because thou also comest in thy mercy to those who need thee most, even to the lost.

And who, think you, will love him best and so reward him best if he comes to them? The proud pharisee in his perfection of imaginary holiness, will he value the Christ who tells him that he comes to wash away his sin? He turns upon his heel with scorn. What sin has he to wash away? The self-satisfied moralist who dares to say, 'All these commands I have kept from my youth up: what lack I yet?' – is he likely to become a disciple of the Great Teacher whose first lessons are, 'Ye must be born again,' and 'Except ye be converted and become as little children, ye shall in no wise enter the kingdom of heaven?' The fact is that Jesus has no form or comeliness to those who have a beauty of their own. Christ finds most love where he pardons most sin; and the sweetest obedience to his command is rendered by those who once were most disobedient, but who are gently led beneath his sway by the force of grateful love. Yon sterile hills of fancied holiness yield him no harvest, and therefore he leaves them to their own boastfulness, but mean-while he scatters plenteous grain amongst the lowlands where the ground is broken and lies ready for the seed. He preaches pardon to those who know that they have sinned, and confess the same: but those who have no sin have no Saviour.

But after all, dear friends, if Jesus did direct his mission of salvation to the lost, to whom else could he have come? For, truth to say, there are none but the lost on the face of this whole earth. The proudest pharisee is but a sinner, and all the more a sinner for his pride; and the moralist who thinks himself so clean is filthy in the sight of God. Though he labours to conceal the spots, the self-righteous man is a leper, and will for ever remain so unless Jesus cleanses him. It is a thrice blessed fact that Christ came to save the lost, for such are we all, and had he not made lost ones the object of his searching and saving, there would have been no hope for us.

What is meant by *'the lost'*? Well, 'lost' is a dreadful word. I should need much time to explain it; but if the Spirit of God, like a flash of light, shall enter into your heart, dear reader, and show you what you are by nature, you will read that word 'lost' as descriptive of your condition, and understand it better than a thousand words of mine could enable you to do. Lost by the fall; lost by inheriting a depraved nature; lost by our own acts and deeds; lost by a thousand omissions of duty, and lost by countless deeds of overt transgression; lost by habits of sin; lost by tendencies and inclinations which have gathered strength and dragged you downward into yet deeper and deeper darkness and iniquity; lost by inclinations which never turn of themselves to that which is right, but which resolutely refuse divine mercy and infinite love. We are lost wilfully and willingly; lost perversely and utterly; but still lost of our own accord, which is the worst kind of being lost that possibly can be. We are lost to God, who has lost our heart's love, and lost our confidence, and lost our obedience; lost to the church which we cannot serve; lost to truth which we will not see; lost to right whose cause we do not uphold; lost to heaven, into whose sacred precincts we can never come; lost – so lost that unless Almighty mercy intervene, we shall be cast into the pit that is bottomless to sink for ever. LOST! LOST! LOST! The very word seems to me to be the knell of an impenitent soul. *Lost! Lost! Lost!* I hear the dismal tolling! A soul's funeral is being celebrated! Endless death has befallen an immortal being! It comes up as a dreadful wail from far beyond the boundaries of life and hope, forth from those dreary regions of death and darkness where spirits dwell who would not have Christ to reign over them. From afar I hear it, and its sound causes my very heart to tremble. *'Lost! Lost! Lost!'* Ah me! That ever these ears should hear the sound. Better a whole world on fire than a soul lost! Better every star quenched and yon skies a wreck than a soul lost!

Now, it is for souls that soon will be in that worst of all conditions and are already preparing for it that Jesus came here seeking and saving. What joy is this! In proportion as the grief was heavy the joy is great. If souls can be delivered from going down into such a state, it is a feat worthy of God himself. Glory be to his name!

Now note *the purpose* – He 'came *to seek and to save that which was lost.*' Ah, this is worth preaching – this doctrine that Jesus came to seek and to save sinners. Some people tell me that he came 'to make men salvable' – to put all men into such a condition that it is possible that they may be saved. I believe that men may be saved, but I see no very great wonder in the fact. It does not stir my blood, or incite me to dance for joy. I do not know that it makes even the slightest impresson upon me. I can go to sleep, and I am sure I shall not wake up in the night, and long to get up at once to preach such poor news as that Jesus came to make men salvable. I would not have become a minister to preach so meagre a gospel: but that our Lord came to save men, that is substantial and satisfying news, far exceeding the other. To make men salvable is a skeleton, bones and skin; but to save them is a living blessing. To make men salvable is a farthing blessing, but to save them is wealth untold. They say also that Jesus came into the world to let men be saved if they will. I am glad of that. It is true and good. I believe that every truly willing soul may be saved, yea, such an one is in a measure saved already. If there be a sincere will towards salvation – understand, towards true salvation – that very will indicates that a great change has commenced within the man; and I rejoice that it is written, 'Whosoever will, let him take the water of life freely.' But now just read our text as if it ran thus – 'The Son of man is come that whoever wills to be saved may be saved.' The sense is good, but very feeble! How is the wine mixed with water! But, oh, what flavour, what essence, what marrow, what fatness there is in this – 'The Son of man is come *to seek and to save that which was lost.*' This is the gospel, and the other is but a part of the good news. Again, read the text another way – 'The Son of man is come to help men to save themselves.' This will not do at all. It is something like helping men to march who have no legs, or helping blind men to judge colours, or helping dead men to make themselves alive. Help to those who can do nothing at all is a miserable mockery. No, we cannot have our Bibles altered that way: we will let the text stand as it is, in all its fulness of grace.

Nor is it even possible for us to cut down our text to this – 'The Son of man is come to save those who seek him.' If it ran so, I would bless God for ever for it; for it would be a glorious gospel text even then. There are scriptures which teach that doctrine, and it is a blessed truth for which to be supremely grateful; but my text goes very much further, for it says, 'The Son of man is come to seek and to save that which was lost.' I met with a question and answer the other day – 'Where did the Samaritan woman find the Saviour? She found him at the well.' I do not cavil at that mode of expression; but, mark you, that is not how I should ask the question. I should rather inquire, 'Where did the Saviour find the woman?' For surely, she was not seeking him; I see no indication that she had any such idea in her mind. She was looking after water from the well, and if she had found that, she would have gone home satisfied. No, those are the finders, surely, who are the seekers; and so it must be that Christ found the woman, for he was looking after her. While I bless my Lord that he will save you if you seek him, I am more thankful still that there are men and women whom he will seek as well as save; nay, that there never was a soul saved yet but Christ sought it first. He is the author as well as the finisher of faith. He is the Alpha and the Omega, the beginning and the ending of the work of grace. Let his name be praised for it. The text must stand as it is, and we will adore the length and breadth, the height and depth of the love which has made it true. Successful seeking and complete saving belong to the Son of man: some of us have experienced both. O that all of us might yet do so.

3. Now we pass on, thirdly, to notice a DOUBLE DIFFICULTY.

We see Christ's errand; and we at once perceive that he has come to deal with people who are lost in two senses, and in each sense a miracle of grace is needed for their deliverance. They are so lost that they need

135

saving, but they are also so lost that they need *seeking.*
Persons may be so lost on land or on sea as to need
saving and not seeking; but we were spiritually lost, so
as to need both saving and seeking too. I heard a little
while ago of a party of friends who went to the lakes
of Cumberland and endeavoured to climb the Lang-
dale Pikes. One of the company found the labour of
the ascent too wearisome, and so resolved that he
would go back to the little inn from which they
started. Being a wiser man than some, in his own
esteem, he did not take the winding path by which
they had ascended. He thought he would go straight
down, for he could see the house just below, and
fancied he should pitch upon it all of a sudden, and
show the mountaineers that a straight line is the nearest road. Well, after descending and descending, leap-
ing many a rugged place, he found himself at last on a
ledge from which he could go neither up nor down.
After many vain attempts he saw that he was a
prisoner. In a state of wild terror, he took off his
garments and tore them into shreds to make a line,
and tying the pieces together he let them down, but he
found that they reached nowhere at all in the great
and apparently unfathomable abyss which yawned
below him. So he began to call aloud; but no answer
came from the surrounding hills beyond the echo of
his own voice. He shouted by the half hour together,
but there was no answer, neither was there anyone
within sight. His horror nearly drove him out of his
wits. At last, to his intense joy, he saw a figure move in
the plain below, and he began to shout again. Happily
it was a woman, who, hearing his voice stopped, and
as he called again she came nearer and called out,
'Keep where you are. Do not stir an inch. Keep where
you are.' He was lost, but he no longer needed seeking,
for some friendly shepherds soon saw where he was.

SEEKER AND SAVIOUR OF THE LOST

All he wanted was saving; and so the mountaineers descended with a rope, as they were wont to do when rescuing lost sheep, and soon brought him out of danger. He was lost, but he did not want seeking; they could see where he was.

A month or two ago you must have noticed in the papers an advertisement for a gentleman who had left Wastwater some days before to go over the hills, and had not been heard of since. His friend had to seek him that, if still alive, he might be saved; and there were those who traversed hill and moor to discover him, but they were unable to save him, because they could not find him. If they could have found out where he was I do not doubt that, had he been in the most imminent peril, the bold hillsmen would have risked their lives to rescue him; but, alas, he was never found or saved: his lifeless corpse was the only discovery which was ultimately made. This last is the true image of our deplorable condition; we are by nature lost, so that nothing but seeking and saving together will be of any service to us.

Let us see how our Lord accomplished the *saving*. That has been done, completely done. My dear friends, you and I were lost in the sense of having broken the law of God and having incurred his anger, but Jesus came and took the sin of men upon himself, and as their surety and their substitute he bore the wrath of God, so that God can henceforth be 'just, and yet the justifier of him that believeth in Jesus.' This blessed doctrine of substitution, I would like to die talking of it, and I intend, by divine grace, to live proclaiming it, for it is the keystone of the gospel. Jesus Christ did literally take upon himself the transgression and iniquity of his people, and was made a curse for them, seeing that they had fallen under the wrath of God; and now every soul that believeth in

CHRIST'S GLORIOUS ACHIEVEMENTS

Jesus is saved because Jesus has taken away the penalty and the curse due to sin. In this let us rejoice. Christ has also saved us from the power of Satan. The seed of the woman has bruised the serpent's head, so that Satan's power is broken. Jesus has by his mighty power set us free from hell's horrible yoke by vanquishing the prince of darkness, and has moreover saved us from the power of death, so that to believers it shall not be death to die. Christ has saved us from sin and all its consequences by his most precious death and resurrection.

> 'See God descending in the human frame,
>   The offended suffering in the offender's name:
> All thy misdeeds to him imputed see,
>   And all his righteousness devolved on thee.'

Our Lord's saving work is in this sense finished, but there is always going on in the world his seeking work, and I want you to think of it.

He can save us, blessed be his name. He has nothing more to do in order to save any soul that trusts him. But we have wandered very far away, and are hidden in the wilds of the far country. We are very hungry, and though there is bread enough and to spare, what is the use of it while we are lost to the home in which it is so freely distributed? We are very ragged; there is the best robe, and it is ready to be put on us; but what is the good of it while we are so far away? There are the music and the dancing to make us glad and to cheer us, but what is the use of them while we still tarry among the swine? Here, then, is the great difficulty. Our Lord must find us out, follow our wanderings, and, treating us like lost sheep, he must bear us back upon his shoulders rejoicing.

Many need seeking because they are lost in bad

company. Evil companions get around men and keep them away from hearing the gospel by which men are saved. There is no place to be lost in like a great city. When a man wants to escape the police he does not run to a little village, he hides away in a thickly populated town. So this London has many hiding places where sinners get out of the gospel's way. They lose themselves in the great crowd, and are held captives by the slavish customs of the evil society into which they are absorbed. If they do but relent for a moment, some worldling plucks them by the sleeve and says, 'Let us be merry while we may. What are you so melancholy about?' Satan carefully sets a watch upon his younger servants to prevent their escaping from his hands. These pickets labour earnestly to prevent the man from hearing the good news of salvation lest he should be converted. Sinners therefore need seeking out from among the society in which they are imbedded; they need as much seeking after as the pearls of the Arabian Gulf.

The Lord Jesus Christ in seeking men has to deal with deep-seated prejudices. Many refuse to hear the gospel: they would travel many miles to escape its warning message. Some are too wise, or too rich to have the gospel preached to them. Pity the poor rich! The poor man has many missionaries and evangelists seeking him out, but who goes after the great ones? Some come from the east to worship, but who comes from the west? Many more will find their way to heaven out of the back slums than ever will come out of the great mansions and palaces. Jesus must seek his elect among the rich under great disadvantages, but blessed be his name he does seek them.

See how vices and depraved habits hold the mass of the poorer classes. What a seeking out is needed among working men, for many of them are besotted with drunkenness. Look at the large part of London on the Lord's day: what have the working population been doing? They have been reading the Sunday newspaper, and loafing about the house in their shirt sleeves, and waiting at the posts of the doors – not of wisdom, but of the drink shop. They have been thirsting, but not after righteousness. Bacchus still remaineth the god of this city, and multitudes are lost among the beer barrels and the spirit casks. In such pursuits men waste the blessed Sabbath hours. How shall they be sought out? Yet the Lord Jesus is doing it by his Holy Spirit.

Alas, through their ill ways men's ears are stopped and their eyes are blinded, and their hearts hardened, so that the messengers of mercy have need of great patience. It were easy work to save men, if they could but be made willing to receive the gospel, but they will not even hear it. When you do get them for a Sabbathday beneath the sound of a faithful ministry, how they struggle against it. They want seeking out fifty times over. You bring them right up to the light, and flash it upon their eyes, but they wilfully and deliberately close their eyelids to it. You set before them life and death, and plead with them even unto tears that they would lay hold on eternal life; but they choose their own delusions. So long and so patiently must they be sought that this seeking work as much reveals the gracious heart of Jesus as did the saving work which he fulfilled upon the bloody tree.

Notice how he is daily accomplishing his search of love. Every day, beloved, Jesus Christ is seeking men's *ears*. Would you believe it? He has to go about with wondrous wisdom even to get a hearing. They do not want to know the love message of their God. 'God so loved the world' – they know all about that, and do not want to hear any more. There is an infinite sacrifice for sin: they turn on their heel at such stale news. They would rather read an article in an infidel Review or a paragraph in the *Police News*. They want to know no more of spiritual matters. The Lord Jesus, in order to get at their ears, cries aloud by many earnest voices. Thank God, he has ministers yet alive who mean to be heard and will not be put off with denials. Even the din of this noisy world cannot drown their testimony. Cry aloud, my brother; cry aloud and spare not, for, cry as you may, you will not cry too loudly, for man will not hear if he can help it. Our Lord, to win men's ears, must use a variety of voices, musical or rough, as his wisdom judges best. Sometimes he gains an audience by an odd voice whose quaintness wins attention. He will reach men when he means to save them. That was an odd voice, surely the oddest I ever heard of, which came a little time ago in an Italian town to one of God's elect ones there. He was so depraved that he actually fell to worshipping the devil rather than God. It chanced one day that a rumour went through the city that a Protestant was coming there to preach. The priest, alarmed for his religion, told the people from the altar that Protestants worshipped the devil, and he charged them not to go near the meeting-room. The news, as you may judge, excited no horror in the devil-worshipper's mind. 'Ay,' thought he, 'then I shall meet with brethren' and so he went to hear our beloved missionary who is now labouring in Rome. Nothing else would have drawn this poor wretch to hear the good word, but this lie of the priest's was overruled to that end. He went and heard, not of the devil, but of the devil's conqueror, and before long was found at Jesus' feet, a sinner saved.

I have known my Lord, when his ministers have failed, take out an arrow from his quiver and fix upon it a message, and put it to his bow, and shoot it right into a man's bosom till it wounded him; and, as it wounded him, and he lay moaning upon his bed, the message has been learned, and felt, and accepted. I mean that many a man in sickness has been brought to hear the message of salvation. Often losses and crosses have brought men to Jesus' feet. Jesus seeks them so. When Absalom could not get an interview with Joab, he said, 'Go and set his barley field on fire.' Then Joab came down to Absalom and said, 'Wherefore have they servants set my barley field on fire?' The Lord sometimes sends losses of property to men who will not otherwise hear him, and at last their ears are gained. Whom he seeketh he in due time findeth.

Well, after my Lord has sought men's ears he next seeks their *desires*. He will have them long for a Saviour, and this is not an easy thing to accomplish; but he has a way of showing men their sins, and then they wish for mercy. He shows them at other times the great joy of the Christian life, and then they wish to enter into the like delight. I pray that, at this hour, he may lead some of you to consider the danger you are in while you are yet unconverted, that so you may begin to desire Christ, and in this way may be sought and found by him.

Then he seeks their *faith*. He seeks that they may come and trust him; and he has ways of bringing them to this, for he shows them the suitability of his salvation, and the fulness and the freeness of it; and when he has exhibited himself as a sinner's Saviour, and such a Saviour as they want, then do they come and put their trust in him. Then has he found them and saved them. All this does his Holy Spirit work in men for their eternal good.

He seeks their *hearts*, for it is their hearts that he has lost. And oh, how sweetly does Christ by the Holy

Spirit, win men's affections and hold them fast. I shall never forget how he won mine, how first he gained my ear, and then my desires, so that I wished to have him for my Lord; and then he taught me to trust him, and when I had trusted him and found that I was saved, then I loved him and I love him still. So, dear hearer, if Jesus Christ shall find you, you will become his loving follower for ever. I have been praying that he would bring this message under the notice of those whom he means to bless. I have asked him to let me sow in good soil. I hope that among those who read these pages there will be many whom the Lord Jesus has specially redeemed with his most precious blood, and I trust that he will appear at once to them, and say, 'I have loved thee with an everlasting love, therefore with loving-kindness have I drawn thee.' By grace omnipotent may you be made to yield to the Lord with the cheerful consent of your conquered wills, and accept that glorious grace which will bring you to praise the seeking and saving Saviour in heaven.

The Spurgeon Collection

The Saint and His Saviour

Till He Come

Faith

The King's Highway

Around the Wicket Gate

John Ploughman's Talk

John Ploughman's Pictures

Come Ye Children

All of Grace

Christ's Glorious Achievements